Henry Wakeham Purkis

The Student's Guide to Williams on Personal Property

Being a Complete Series of Questions and Answers

Henry Wakeham Purkis

The Student's Guide to Williams on Personal Property
Being a Complete Series of Questions and Answers

ISBN/EAN: 9783337402235

Printed in Europe, USA, Canada, Australia, Japan

Cover: Foto ©Suzi / pixelio.de

More available books at **www.hansebooks.com**

THE STUDENT'S GUIDE

TO

WILLIAMS ON PERSONAL PROPERTY.

BEING

A COMPLETE SERIES

OF

QUESTIONS AND ANSWERS THEREON.

BY

H. WAKEHAM PURKIS, Esq.,

AUTHOR OF "THE STUDENT'S GUIDE TO WILLIAMS ON REAL PROPERTY," "THE
STUDENT'S GUIDE TO SMITH ON CONTRACTS."

———————

PHILADELPHIA:

T. & J. W. JOHNSON & CO.,

LAW BOOKSELLERS AND PUBLISHERS,

No. 535 CHESTNUT STREET.

1882.

TABLE OF CONTENTS.

INTRODUCTORY CHAPTER.

PART I.

OF CHOSES IN POSSESSION.

PART II.

OF CHOSES IN ACTION.

PART III.

OF INCORPOREAL PERSONAL PROPERTY.

iv   CONTENTS.

PART IV.

OF PERSONAL ESTATE GENERALLY.

PART V.

ANSWERS TO QUESTIONS

WILLIAMS' LAW OF PERSONAL PROPERTY.

INTRODUCTORY CHAPTER.

OF THE SUBJECTS AND NATURE OF PERSONAL PROPERTY.

Q. Into what two great branches is the English law of property divided, and how was it anciently divided?

A. Into the law of real property and the law of personal property. The feudal rules which respected the holding and culture of land were the elements of the common law of real property; the rules relating to the disposition of goods were the origin of the law of personal property, which was, however, subject to the civil law in case of transmission by will or intestacy. The division of property into real and personal is comparatively of modern date. In ancient times property was divided into lands, tenements and hereditaments on the one hand, and goods and chattels on the other.

Q. Into how many classes were actions divided? Name them, and specify the nature of each.

A. Into real, personal and mixed. Real actions were brought for the recovery of lands; personal

P. Prop.   1

actions were brought in respect of *goods;* and mixed actions were for real and personal mixed together.

Q. In what two personal actions could the identical goods be recovered?

A. In actions of detinue and in replevin.

Q. What is a chose in action, and was it assignable at law?

A. It is a right of action, or the liberty of proceeding in the courts of law to recover pecuniary damages for the infliction of a wrong or the non-performance of a contract, or to procure the payment of money due. Choses in action, with few exceptions, could not formerly be transferred.

Q. What alteration has been made by the Judicature Act, 1873, as to the assignment of debts or other legal choses in action?

A. It is provided that any absolute assignment by writing, under the hand of the assignor (not purporting to be by way of charge only), of any debt or other legal chose in action, of which express notice in writing shall have been given to the person from whom the assignor would have been entitled to receive or claim such debt or chose in action, shall be effectual at law (subject to all equities which would have been entitled to priority over the right of the assignee if this Act had not been passed) to pass the legal right to such debt or chose in action from the date of such notice, and all legal and other remedies for the same, and the power to give a good discharge for the same without the concurrence of the assignor.

Q. What were equitable choses in action?

A. Rights which, prior to the Supreme Court of Judicature Acts, 1873 and 1875, were enforceable only by suit in equity; as, for instance, a pecuniary legacy, for which, if the executor withheld payment, the legatee could maintain no action at law, but must resort to equity. This kind of chose in action might have been assigned directly from one person to another, and the assignee might sue in equity in his own name.

Q. How does personal property differ from real?

A. Personal property is distinguished from real by being unaffected by the feudal rules of tenure, by being alienable by methods altogether different, by passing in the first instance to the executors when bequeathed by will, and by devolving, in case of intestacy, not upon the heir, but on an administrator (appointed formerly by the Ecclesiastical Court, afterwards by the Court of Probate, and now by the Probate, Divorce and Admiralty Division of the High Court of Justice), by whom it is distributed amongst the next of kin of the deceased. Personal property also differs essentially from real in that it is the subject of absolute ownership, whereas there is no such thing as an absolute ownership in real property; the utmost that can be enjoyed in real property is an estate for life, or an estate tail, or an estate in fee simple.

PART I.

OF CHOSES IN POSSESSION.

CHAPTER I.

OF CHATTELS WHICH DESCEND TO THE HEIR.

Q. What are choses in possession, and what choses in possession (or chattels) form exceptions to the general rule as to their devolution?

A. Movable goods, such as plate, furniture, farming stock (both live and dead), locomotive engines, ships, &c., which are essentially the subjects of absolute ownership and cannot be held by estates. The chattels which form exceptions to the general rule, as to their devolution, consist principally of *title deeds, heirlooms, fixtures, chattels vegetable,* and *animals feræ naturæ.*

Q. What are heirlooms, and upon whom do they devolve on the decease of the owner?

A. Heirlooms are such personal chattels as go, by force of a *special custom,* to the heir and not to the executor or administrator of the last owner, who, if he leaves the land to descend to his heir, cannot by his will bequeath the heirloom. The ancient jewels of the crown are heirlooms; also coat armor, tombstones, and boxes in which muniments of title are kept. In popular language the term "heirloom" is generally applied to plate, pictures or articles of property which have been assigned by deed of settlement or bequeathed by will, in trust and for the use and enjoyment of the person for the time being in possession of the mansion house in which the articles may be placed.

Q. What are fixtures in the ordinary acceptance of the term, and what is the maxim as to them?

A. Fixtures are such movable articles or chattels personal as are fixed to the ground or soil, either directly or indirectly, by being attached to a house or other building, the motto being "*quicquid plantatur solo, solo cedit.*" A conveyance or a mortgage of a house or other building will comprise all ordinary fixtures, such as stoves, grates, shelves, locks, &c., and also fixtures erected for the purposes of trade, unless an intention to the contrary is expressed or may be gathered from the context. So, on the decease of a tenant in fee simple, the devisee of a house, or the heir at law in case of intestacy, will be entitled generally to the fixtures set up on it.

Q. What are agricultural fixtures, and in what respect was the old rule relaxed in favor of the tenant by stat. 14 & 15 Vict. c. 25, s. 3, also by the Agricultural Holdings Act, 1875?

A. The old rule that agricultural fixtures, though set up by the tenant, became, by being fixed to the soil, the property of the landlord, was relaxed in favor of the tenant by stat. 14 & 15 Vict. c. 25, s. 3, which provides that fixtures put up with the consent *in writing* of the landlord shall be removable by the tenant on his giving the landlord or his agent one month's previous notice in writing of his intention so to do, subject to the landlord's right to purchase the same by valuation in the

manner provided by that Act. A further relaxation
of the old rule has been made by the Agricultural Holdings (England) Act, 1875 (38 & 39 Vict. c. 92), in favor
of the tenant; but the application of the Act may be
totally or partially excluded by agreement between the
landlord and tenant, and it does not apply to holdings
that are not agricultural or pastoral, or of less extent
than two acres. A further relaxation of the old rule
has also been made in favor of the executors of a tenant
for life, who appear to be allowed to remove fixtures set
up by their testator for the purposes of trade or of ornament or domestic convenience.

Q. What are emblements, and to whom do they
descend?

A. Such vegetable products as are the annual results
of agricultural labor are called *emblements*, and the right
to reap them belongs to the executor or administrator
of a deceased owner in fee, in exclusion of the heir (but
not of a devisee of the land). Crops of corn and grain
of all kinds, flax, hemp, and everything yielding an
annual profit produced by labor, belong to the executor
or administrator as against the heir; whilst timber, fruit,
trees, grass and clover, which do not repay within the
year the labor by which they are produced, belong to
the heir as part of the land. The right to emblements
also belongs to the executor or administrator of a tenant
for life, and to a tenant at will if dismissed from his
tenancy before harvest.

Q. What trees are considered as timber?

A. Oak, ash and elm in all places, and in some particular parts of the country, by local custom, where

other trees are generally used for building, they are for that reason considered as timber.

Q. What are animals *feræ naturæ?*

A. Animals *feræ naturæ*, or wild animals, including game, are exceptions from the rules which relate to other movables, as until they are caught there is no property in them. If, therefore, the owner of land in fee simple dies, the game on his land, or the fish in any pond or river upon his land, will not belong to his executor or administrator. But a property in wild animals may be obtained by reclaiming or catching them, or by reason of their being unable to get away; as deer in a park, rabbits in a hutch, &c., which will belong to the executor or administrator and not the heir.

Q. Who has the right to kill and take game?

A. The occupier of land for the time being has the sole right of killing and taking the game upon the land, unless such right be reserved to the landlord or any other person. Where the landlord has reserved to himself the right of killing game he may authorize any person who has a license to kill game to enter upon the land for the purpose of pursuing and killing game thereon. And the lord of any manor has the right to pursue and kill the game upon the waste or commons within the manor, and to authorize any other person or persons who shall hold a license to kill game to enter upon such wastes or commons for the same purpose.

Q. In whom does the property in dead game vest?

A. Under the provisions of the Game Act (1 & 2 Will. 4, c. 32) the property in game killed on any land by strangers vests in the person having the right to kill and take game upon the land.

CHAPTER II.

OF TROVER, BAILMENT, AND LIEN.

Q. Define an action of trover and *conversion*, and for what it is usually brought, and when can it be maintained.

A. The word *trover* is from the French *trouver*, to find; and the word *conversion* is added, from the conversion of the goods to the use of the defendant, being the gist of the action thus brought against him. That defendant should have found the article lost is not his fault, but his conversion of it to his own use is a trespass, and renders him liable to an action for trover and conversion, which action is now constantly brought to recover damages for withholding the possession of goods wrongfully diverted by defendant to his own use, without regard to the means, whether by finding or otherwise, by which defendant may have become possessed. Several alterations in the mode of procedure have been effected by the Judicature Act, 1875; and this action can be maintained only when the plaintiff has been in possession of the goods, or has such a property in them as draws to it the right to the possession.

Q. Define bailment, and give some instances, and state in whom the property in the goods delivered remains.

A. Bailment is a delivery of goods in trust on a contract expressed or implied that the trusts shall be duly executed and the goods redelivered as soon as the trust or use for which they were bailed shall have elapsed or be performed; as, for instance, if lent to a friend, or left in the custody of a warehouseman or wharfinger, or entrusted to a carrier or to an agent or factor to sell. The term *bailment* is derived from the French word *bailler*, to deliver. The person who delivers the goods is called the bailor, the person to whom the goods are delivered the *bailee*. In all cases of bailment the simple rule still holds that the property in goods can belong to one party only, and when any goods are *bailed* the property still remains in the bailor.

Q. In the case of a simple bailment who may maintain an action for trover? and what is the difference in this respect if the bailment is not of the simple kind?

A. A bailee may maintain this action, because the action depends only on the right to the possession which the bailee has by virtue of the bailment made to him; and the bailor may also maintain the action, because his property in the goods draws with it the right of possession, and the bailment is not of such a kind as to vest this right in the bailee solely. If, however, the bailment should not be of the simple kind, but should confer on the bailee the right to exclude the bailor from the possession, here, though the property in the goods still remains in the bailor, the bailee alone can maintain an action of trover against any person who may have taken the goods and converted them to his own use. Thus the pawnee, or hirer of goods, can alone maintain an action of trover so long as the pawning or hiring continues.

Q. Define a lien. What are the two kinds? and give instances.

A. A lien is the right of a person in the possession of goods to retain them until a debt due to him has been satisfied. A lien is either *particular* or *general*. A particular lien is a right to retain the particular goods in respect of which the debt arises. A general lien is a right to retain goods in respect of a general balance of an account. The former kind is favored in law; but the latter, having a tendency to prefer one creditor above another, is taken strictly. A particular lien is given by the common law over goods which a person is compelled to receive; thus carriers and innkeepers have a lien on goods in their care. A particular lien is also given by law to every person who by his labor or skill has improved or altered an article entrusted to his care. A general lien, when it does not arise by express contract or from a contract implied by the course of dealing between the parties, accrues by custom of some trade or profession, and it may be local also. It obtains in many trades, such as wharfingers, dyers, calico printers, factors, bankers, and perhaps, also, common carriers. Solicitors also have a lien on all the deeds and documents of their clients in their possession for their professional charges generally.

Q. What is the effect of 23 & 24 Vict. c. 127, s. 28, as to solicitors' charges?

A. When a solicitor is employed to prosecute or defend any suit, matter, or proceeding, in any court of justice, the court or judge before whom it has been heard or is depending may declare such solicitor entitled to a charge upon the property recovered or preserved, which will operate as a charge upon such property for

the taxed costs, charges, and expenses of or in reference to such suit, matter, or proceeding.

Q. How is a lien lost?

A. A lien of whatever kind is merely a right to retain the *possession* of the goods, but the *property* in the
goods still remains with the owner; and if the person
having the lien should give up possession of his goods
his lien will be lost, and the owner's property in them
will draw to it the right of possession, and enable him to
maintain an action of trover. And if the person having the lien should take a security for his debt, payable
at a distant day, his lien would on that account be lost,
as it would be unreasonable that he should detain the
goods till such future time of payment.

CHAPTER III.

OF THE ALIENATION OF CHOSES IN POSSESSION.

Q. How may the property in goods to be hereafter
acquired be effectually passed?

A. By an assignment thereof in equity, coupled with
a license to seize them.

Q. By what modes are personal chattels alienable?

A. Personal chattels are still alienable by mere *gift
and delivery*, though they may be disposed of by *deed;*
and they are also assignable by sale in a manner totally
different from the conveyance requisite on the transfer
of real estate.

Q. In what respect does a contract for the sale of chattels personal differ from a contract for the sale of real property?

A. In the case of a contract for the sale of chattels personal, such a contract immediately transfers the legal property in the goods sold from the vendor to the vendee. In order to do this it is of course necessary that the transaction have within itself all the legal requisites for a sale.

Q. What are the requisites for the sale of goods under the value of 10*l.*?

A. There can be no sale without a tender or part payment of the money, or a tender or part delivery of the goods, unless the contract is to be completed at a future time.

Q. When does the property in the goods pass to the purchaser?

A. If the sale is valid the property will pass at once from the vendor to the vendee, but if any act remains to be done on the part of the seller previously to the delivery of the goods, the property does not pass to the vendee until such act is done. Thus, if goods, the weight of which is unknown, are sold by weight, or if a given weight or measure is sold out of a larger quantity, the property will not pass to the vendee until the price shall have been ascertained by weighing the goods in the one case, or the goods sold shall have been separated by weight or measure in the other.

Q. What are the requisites for the sale of goods of the value of 10*l.* or upwards?

A. By the Statute of Frauds (sect. 17), " no such contract for the sale of any goods, wares or merchandises will be good, except the buyer accept part of the goods so sold, and actually receive the same, or give something in earnest to bind the bargain or in part payment, or some note or memorandum in writing of the said bargain is signed by the parties to be charged by such contract or their agents thereunto lawfully authorized."

Q. What is an actual acceptance and actual receipt within the statute?

A. There must be an actual transfer of the article sold, or some part thereof, by the seller, and an actual taking possession of it by the buyer. So, if any part of the goods be delivered to an agent of the vendee, or to a carrier named by him, this is a sufficient receipt by the vendee himself; if the goods are in the possession of a warehouseman or wharfinger, the receipt of a delivery order is sufficient when the bailee agrees to hold the goods on the purchaser's account.

Q. What is the law as to vendor's lien, with regard to constructive possession?

A. Formerly, so long as vendor retains actual or constructive possession of the goods, he had a lien upon them for so much of the purchase-money as might remain unpaid; but now the law has been altered with regard to constructive possession, and the lien of the vendor is liable to be defeated by the endorsement, or delivery by the vendee, of any document of title to the goods, to a person who takes the same *bonâ fide* and for valuable consideration.

Q. What is stoppage *in transitu*, and when may a vendor or consignor exercise this right?

A. The right of *stoppage in transitu* occurs when goods are consigned wholly or partly on credit from one person to another, and the consignee becomes bankrupt or insolvent before the goods arrive. In this event the consignor has a right to direct the captain of the ship, or other carrier, to deliver the goods to himself or his agent instead of to the consignee, who has thus become unable to pay for them (notice to the holder of the goods is sufficient).

Q. In what case does the property in goods pass from one person to another without any actual sale?

A. In an action of trover, the defendant, when he has paid the amount of the damage, is entitled to retain the goods in respect of which the action is brought, and the property in them vests in him accordingly.

Q. What persons are prohibited from the alienation of personal chattels, and what is the effect of the Naturalization Act, 1870, as regards aliens?

A. Until recently, an *alien* or foreigner was under great restrictions as to the acquirement of real estate; but with respect to both real estate and personal chattels he now stands on the same footing as a natural-born subject, by the Naturalization Act, 1870 (33 Vict. c. 19); and a title to real and personal property of every description may be derived through, from or in succession to him.

Q. In what case does property become forfeited to the crown, and what alteration has been made in the law of forfeiture by the stat. 33 & 34 Vict. c. 23?

A. Where a person is outlawed, or put out of the protection of the law, his property becomes forfeited to the crown. Formerly all personal property which accrued to a felon during his transportation was forfeited to the crown, but a mere contingent interest was not forfeited if it did not vest until the expiration of the period of banishment. But the recent Act (33 & 34 Vict. c. 23, passed 4th July, 1870) enacts that, after its passing, no confession, verdict, inquest, conviction or judgment of or for any treason or felony or *felo de se*, shall cause any attainder or corruption of blood, or any forfeiture or escheat: provided that nothing in the Act shall affect the law of forfeiture consequent upon outlawry.

Q. In what case is the alienation of personal chattels void?

A. By stat. 13 Eliz. c. 5, the gift of any lands, tenements, hereditaments, *goods and chattels*, made for the purpose of delaying, hindering or defrauding creditors, is rendered void, as against them, unless made upon *good*, which here means *valuable*, consideration, and *bonâ fide* to any person not having at the time of such gift notice of such fraud.

Q. In the case of a mortgage of goods, with whom does the right of possession of property vest, where there is a proviso for quiet enjoyment until default?

A. The right of possession vests in the mortgagor until default, but the property in the goods passes at law by the deed to the mortgagee, who cannot maintain an action of trover for the goods against a stranger until default has been made. In the case of a pledge the property remains with the pledgor, and the right to possession with the pledgee.

Q. What are the principal requisites in a bill of sale

under the Bills of Sale Acts, 17 & 18 Vict. c. 36 and 38 & 39 Vict. c. 96?

A. Under the former Act, every bill of sale, whereby the grantee has power to take possession of any effects therein comprised, must be registered in the office of the Court of Queen's Bench within twenty-one days, by filing the same or a copy thereof in that office; otherwise such bill of sale is rendered void, so far as regards any of the goods in the apparent possession of the grantor, as against the creditors of the grantor, in case of his bankruptcy, and as against the assignees under any assignment for the benefit of his creditors, and as against all sheriff's officers and other persons seizing the effects in execution of any process of law or equity issued against the goods of the grantor. It was also enacted by the 29 & 30 Vict. c. 96 that a bill of sale must be duly stamped before it can be registered, and that such registration must be renewed every five years.(a)

(a) The recent Act (41 & 42 Vict. c. 31), which comes into operation on the 1st January, 1879, applies to all bills of sale of "personal chattels" made on or after that date. Fixtures and growing crops are to be comprised in the term "personal chattels" (when separately assigned or charged), but not chattel interests in real estate, nor fixtures (except trade machinery), when assigned together with a freehold or leasehold interest in any land or building; and personal chattels shall be deemed to be in the "apparent possession" of the assignor so long as they remain on the premises occupied or used by him, notwithstanding formal possession by any other person. Trade machinery is to be deemed "personal chattels," but the term "trade machinery" is not to include fixed *motive-power*, as steam-engines, water-wheels, &c.; nor fixed *power machinery*, as shafts, wheels, drums, &c.; nor pipes for steam, gas and water.

Q. What is a writ of fi. fa., and when does it bind the goods?

A. When a creditor takes proceedings against his debtor a sale of the debtor's goods and chattels may be procured by a writ of fi. fa. issued in *execution* of the *judgment* of the court. This writ directs the sheriff to cause the debt to be realized out of the goods and chattels of the debtor, and a sale of the goods is made by the sheriff accordingly. By stat. 19 & 20 Vict. c. 97, s. 1, it is provided that no writ of execution shall prejudice the title to goods acquired by any person *bonâ fide* and for a valuable consideration, before the actual *seizure* thereof by virtue of such writ; provided such person had not, at the time when he acquired such title, notice that a writ had been delivered to the officer and remained unexecuted.

Q. What is a writ of elegit, and what goods are exempted from execution under this writ?

A. By the writ of *elegit* the goods of the debtor are delivered to his creditor at an appraised value, together with possession of his lands; but the wearing apparel and bedding of any judgment debtor or his family, and

---

This Act also provides that the execution of every bill of sale must be attested by a solicitor, and the attestation must state that before execution the effect thereof was explained to the grantor by such solicitor. It must now be registered within seven clear days after the making or giving thereof. In case two or more bills of sale are given comprising any of the same chattels they will take effect according to priority of registration. A transfer of a registered bill of sale need not be registered. Chattels comprised in a bill of sale, duly registered, shall not be within the order and disposition clause of the Bankruptcy Act, 1869.

the tools and implements of his trade (not exceeding in the whole the value of 5*l.*), are not liable to seizure under any execution or order.

Q. What property of a bankrupt now comes within the order and disposition clause?

A. By the Bankruptcy Act, 1869 (32 & 33 Vict. c. 71), the property of a bankrupt divisible among his creditors comprises all goods and chattels being at the commencement of the bankruptcy in the possession, order, or disposition of the bankrupt, *being a trader*, by the consent and permission of the true owner, or of which goods and chattels the bankrupt is reputed owner, or of which he has taken upon himself the sale or disposition as owner; provided that things in action, other than debts due to him in the course of his trade or business, shall not be deemed goods and chattels within the meaning of that clause. Registration of a bill of sale now takes the property comprised in it out of the order and disposition clause. (*b*)

CHAPTER IV.

OF SHIPS.

Q. Into how many shares is the property in every British ship divided?

A. Into sixty-four shares; and subject to the provisions of the Act with respect to joint owners, or

---

(*b*) See note (*a*), *ante*, pp. 16, 17.

owners by transmission, not more than thirty-two individuals shall be entitled to be registered at the same time as owners of any one ship; but this rule is not to affect the beneficial title of any number of persons, or any company represented by or claiming under any registered owner or joint owner.

Q. What is a certificate of registry, and for what purpose is it used?

A. Upon the completion of the registry of any ship the registrar gives a certificate of registry in the forms prescribed by the Act. This certificate is to be used only for the navigation of the ship, and is kept in the custody of the master, and is not subject to detention by reason of any lien, charge, or interest, which any owner, mortgagee, or other person, may claim in the ship described in such certificate.

Q. How are ships or shares in ships transferred?

A. By bill of sale, which must contain such a description of the ship as is contained in the surveyor's certificate, or as may be sufficient to identify the ship to the satisfaction to the registrar, and must be in the form given in the schedule of the Act, or as near thereto as circumstances permit, and executed by the transferor, and attested by one or more witnesses. And no individual can be registered as transferee of a ship, or any share therein, until he has made a declaration in the form prescribed by the Act, the bill of sale and declaration to be produced to the registrar of the port at which the ship is registered, who enters the name of transferee on the registry, and endorses on the bill of sale the fact of such entry, with the date and hour thereof.

Q. What are the principal provisions of the Merchant Shipping Act as to the mortgage of ships?

A. All mortgages of any ship, or any shares therein, are to be in a form prescribed by the Act, or as near thereto as circumstances permit; and on the production thereof to the registrar of the port where the ship is registered he records the same in the registry. Mortgagees to take priority according to the date of *registration*. The mortgage when discharged must be produced to the registrar, with receipt for the mortgage money endorsed thereon, duly signed and attested, who will enter such discharge in the register book. All instruments used in carrying into effect that part of the Act which relates to British ships, their ownership and registry, are exempt from stamp duty.

Q. What courts of law now have jurisdiction to decide all matters and causes relating to shipping?

A. The jurisdiction of the High Court of Admiralty has now been transferred to the High Court of Justice, and a division of the court has been established for probate, divorce, and admiralty, and some county courts now possess admiralty jurisdiction.

Q. What is a charter-party?

A. When a vessel is hired for a certain term or a given voyage the instrument by which such hiring is effected is called a charter-party.

Q. What is a bill of lading?

A. Where a merchant ship is open to the conveyance of goods generally it is called a *general ship*, and the receipt for the goods given by the master is called the *bill of lading*; which, when endorsed by the consignee with his name, becomes a negotiable instrument, the delivery of which passes the property in the goods.

Q. What is freight? and what are the rights of a mortgagee with regard to it?

A. The money payable for the hire of a ship or for the carriage of goods in it is the *freight*, which is assignable in the same manner as any other ordinary chose in action. But in case of the mortgage of a ship the mortgagee whose mortgage is first registered obtains, by taking actual or constructive possession, a legal right to the freight, with all the advantages which equity gives to a legal owner in the event of a conflict of claims.

PART II.

OF CHOSES IN ACTION.

CHAPTER I.

OF ACTIONS EX DELICTO.

Q. What alterations have been made by the Judicature Acts, 1873 and 1875, in the jurisdiction and division of the several courts?

A. The Supreme Court of Judicature Acts, 1873 (36 & 37 Vict. c. 66) and 1875 (38 & 39 Vict. c. 77, amended by 40 Vict. c. 9), have now merged the Courts of Common Law, and of Chancery, Admiralty, Probate, and Divorce, into one court, called the Supreme Court of Judicature, which consists of two prominent divisions, one of which, under the name of Her Majesty's High Court of Justice, exercises original jurisdiction; and the other, under the name of Her Majesty's Court of Appeal, exercises appellate jurisdiction.

Q. What exclusive power has each division?

A. The High Court of Justice is again divided into five divisions, namely, the Chancery Division, the Queen's Bench Division, the Common Pleas Division, the Exchequer Division, and the Probate, Divorce and Admiralty Division; to each of which are assigned all causes and matters which would have been in the exclusive jurisdiction of each court if the Act had not passed. The Chancery Division has also assigned to it all causes and matters for any of the following purposes: the administration of the estates of deceased persons; the dissolution of partnerships or the taking of partnership or other accounts; the redemption or foreclosure of mortgages; the raising of portions or other charges on land; the sale and distribution of the proceeds of property, subject to any lien or charge; the execution of trusts, charitable or private; the rectification or setting aside or cancellation of deeds or other written instruments; the specific performance of contracts between vendors and purchasers of real estates, including contracts for leases; the partition or sale of real estates; and the wardship of infants and the care of infants' estates. But, subject to these provisions and to any rules of court, and to the power to transfer causes from one division to another, any plaintiff may assign his cause to such one of the divisions of the High Court as he may think fit.

Q. Into what two great classes are personal actions divided?

A. Actions are divided by the law of England into two great classes: actions *ex delicto*, and actions *ex contractu*. The former arise in respect of wrongs committed, called in law French a *tort;* the latter in respect of contracts made for the performance of some action, which thus becomes a *duty*, or for the payment of some money, which thus becomes a *debt*.

Q. What is the ancient maxim which applies in case of the death of either party to an action *ex delicto?* and state exceptions made by recent statutes.

A. The ancient maxim was "*actio personalis moritur cum personâ*," it being formerly held that if either party died, the right of action was at an end. In this rule, actions *ex delicto* only were included. By subsequent statutes this rule has been considerably relaxed; and recently, by 3 & 4 Will. 4, c. 42, the executors or administrators may bring an action within a year of the death for any injury to the real estate of the deceased committed within six months before his death; and by stats. 9 & 10 Vict. c. 93, and 27 & 28 Vict. c. 95, compensation is recoverable by the legal personal representatives of a person whose death has been caused by the wrongful act of another if such action is brought within a year of the death and is for the benefit of wife, husband, parent or child of the deceased.

Q. State, generally, the law as to the liability of the representatives of a deceased incumbent in estimating the amount of dilapidations.

A. The incumbent is bound to maintain the parsonage, farm buildings and chancel in good and substantial repair; but he is not bound to supply or maintain anything in the nature of ornament. And no damages can be recovered on account of neglect to cultivate the glebe lands in a husbandlike manner. Where any part of the premises were in the occupation of a tenant who was liable to repair, the executors of the incumbent were exempt from liability by the ancient canon law. And the Ecclesiastical Dilapidations Act, 1871 (34 & 35 Vict. c. 43, s. 58), accordingly exempts from its provisions buildings (if any) belonging to a benefice, which shall be comprised in any lease for years or lives for the time being subsisting, except so far as the lessee shall not, by virtue of such lease, be liable to insure, rebuild or repair such buildings. The *new* incumbent was formerly bound to expend within two years the money recovered by him for dilapidations in the necessary repairs of the premises. But he is now bound forthwith to pay the money recovered to the governors of Queen Anne's Bounty, who expend it on the works according to the certificate of the Surveyor of Dilapidations.

Q. What alteration as to payment of dilapidations is made by the Ecclesiastical Dilapidations Act, 1871?

A. It is now provided by 34 & 35 Vict. c. 43, s. 36, that the cost of the repairs shall be a debt due from the late incumbent, his executors or administrators, to the new incumbent, and shall be recoverable as such at law or in equity; formerly they were only payable after all other debts had been paid.

CHAPTER II.

OF CONTRACTS.

Q. In case of an action for damages, by whom are such damages ascertained?

A. The Common Law Procedure Act, 1852 (15 & 16 Vict. c. 76, s. 94), provides that in actions in which it shall appear to the court or a judge that the amount of damages sought to be recovered by the plaintiff is substantially a matter for calculation, the court or a judge may direct that the amount for which final judgment is to be signed shall be ascertained by one of the masters of the court.

Q. What are liquidated damages? State the difference between them and unliquidated damages.

A. Liquidated damages occur in the case of a contract where parties agree between themselves that in the event of a breach by either party a given sum shall be recovered from him by the other as stipulated or liquidated damages, and in this case the whole of the sum thus agreed on may be recovered from the defaulter on a breach of the contract. But where a sum of money is stipulated to be recovered as liquidated damages in case of the breach of an agreement to do several acts, and such sum will, in case of breaches of the agreement, be in some instances too large, and in others too small, as compensation for the injury occasioned, such stipulated sum will not be allowed to be recovered in case of any breach, but damages only, proportioned to the actual injury caused by such breach, unless the parties have contracted, in clear and express terms, that for the breach of each and every stipulation contained in the agreement a sum certain is to be paid, when the parties will be held to their contract.

Q. Define a contract.

A. A contract, as defined by Blackstone, is "an agreement upon consideration to do or not to do a particular thing." This agreement may be either express or implied; for the law always implies a promise to do that which a person is legally liable to perform, and the action of *assumpsit* on promises is constantly maintained for damages for the breach of such an implied contract. Thus, the person who takes the goods of a tradesman is liable in *assumpsit* for their market value; for, as he took the goods, the law will imply for him a promise to pay for them.

Q. How is every action now commenced in the High Court of Justice?

A. By writ of summons, on which is endorsed a short statement of the claim made according to forms given in the Appendix (A), Parts I. and II., to the Supreme Court of Judicature Act, 1875.

Q. What is the difference between simple contracts and special contracts?

A. Express contracts are either by parol or word of mouth, which are called *simple contracts,* or by deed under seal, which are called *special contracts;* although simple contracts may, and often must, at the present day, be evidenced by writing.

Q. Into what two classes are considerations divided? Define them.

A. Into *good* and *valuable.* A good consideration is that of *blood,* or the natural love and affection which a person has for his children or any of his relatives. A valuable consideration is either pecuniary or the gift or conveyance of anything valuable; or it may be in consideration of marriage, or the compromise of a *bonâ fide* claim, &c.; but a *good* consideration is not good for very much in law, and is not good as against creditors within the statute 13 Eliz. c. 5; it is not good to support a contract; and a gift for such consideration is regarded as simply voluntary.

Q. What consideration is necessary to support a valid contract?

A. A valuable consideration is in all cases necessary to form a valid contract. It has been thought that an express promise, founded on a moral obligation, is sufficient for this purpose. This, however, appears to be a mistake. An express promise can give no original right of action if the obligation on which it is founded could never have been itself enforced. But in some cases a valuable consideration, which might have formed a contract by means of an implied promise had its operation not been suspended by some positive rule of law, may be revived and made available by a subsequent express promise.

Q. How may a debt barred by the Statute of Limitations be revived?

A. A simple contract debt, which would otherwise have been barred by the Statute of Limitations from having been incurred upwards of six years, may be revived by a subsequent promise to pay, or even by an unconditional acknowledgment of the debt.

Q. Can a contract by an infant be confirmed after his coming of age?

A. Formerly it might by writing signed by him under Lord Tenterden's Act, 9 Geo. 4, c. 14; but the law as to the contracts of infants has been amended by the Infants Relief Act, 1874 (37 & 38 Vict. c. 62, s. 1), which provides that all contracts, whether by specialty or simple contract, henceforth entered into by infants for the repayment of money lent or to be lent, or for goods supplied or to be supplied (other than contracts for necessaries), and all accounts stated with infants, shall be absolutely void. But this enactment is not to invalidate any contract into which an infant may, by any existing or future statutes, or by the rules of common law or equity, enter, except such as are now by law voidable. The Act also provides (sect. 2) that no action shall be brought to charge any person upon any promise made after full age to pay any debt contracted during infancy, or upon any ratification made after full age, of any promise or contract made during infancy, whether there shall or shall not be any new consideration for such promise or ratification after full age.

Q. What is the effect of the 4th section of the Statute of Frauds?

A. No action can be brought whereby to charge any executor or administrator upon any special promise to answer damages out of his own estate;

Or whereby to charge the defendant upon any special promise to answer for the debt, default or miscarriage of another person;

Or to charge any person upon any agreement made upon consideration of marriage;

Or upon any contract or sale of lands, tenements or hereditaments, or any interest in or concerning them;

Or upon any agreement that is not to be performed within one year from the making thereof;

unless the agreement upon which such action shall be brought, or some memorandum or note thereof, shall be in writing, and signed by the party to be charged therewith, or some other person thereunto by him lawfully authorized.

Q. Cite one or two important cases which have been decided upon the above section.

A. One of the most important is that of *Wain* v. *Warlters*, 5 East, 10; 2 Smith's Leading Cases, 147, in which it was held that the statute in requiring the *agreement* to be in writing required that the *consideration* should be in writing as well as the promise itself. And therefore a promise in writing to pay the debt of a third person, which did not state any *consideration*, was held to give no cause of action, and parol evidence of a consideration was not allowable. And see *Clancy* v. *Piggott*, 1 Smith's Leading Cases, 136.

Q. What alteration has been made by the 19 & 20 Vict. c. 97, s. 3, as to guarantees?

A. That no guarantee shall be invalid to support an action, by reason only that the *consideration* for such promise does not appear in writing, or by necessary inference from a written document. See the cases of *Holmes* v. *Mitchell*, 7 C. B., N. S. 361; *Williams* v. *Lake*, 2 Ell. & Ell. 349.

Q. What is the effect of stat. 9 Geo. 4, c. 14, s. 7, commonly called Lord Tenterden's Act, with regard to the Statute of Limitations?

A. By this statute no acknowledgment or promise by words only can take any case of simple contract out of the operation of the Statute of Limitations, unless it be made or contained by or in some writing to be signed by the party chargeable thereby. The statute makes no mention of any signature by an agent; but by stat. 19 & 20 Vict. c. 97, s. 13, the signature of an agent has been rendered sufficient in this case.

Q. How does the stat. 19 & 20 Vict. c. 97 affect the contracts of co-contractors ?

A. By this statute payment of any principal or interest by a co-contractor or co-debtor will not deprive a debtor of the benefit of the Statute of Limitations.

Q. Can an action be sustained upon a representation as to the character, conduct or ability of another ?

A. If made with the intent that such person may obtain credit, money or goods *upon;* but the party making it will not be liable unless it is made in writing and is signed by him (9 Geo. 4, c. 14).

Q. Define a bill of exchange.

A. A bill of exchange is a written order from one person to another to pay to a third person, or to his order, or to the bearer, a certain sum of money. The person making the order is called the drawer, the person on whom it is made the drawee, and the person to whom the money is payable the payee. The bill is sometimes made payable to the drawer himself, or to his order, or to him or bearer. If the person on whom the bill is drawn undertakes to pay it he writes on it the word "accepted," with his signature, and is then called the acceptor.(a) A promissory note (or note of hand) is a written promise from one person to pay to another, or to his order, or to bearer, a certain sum of money. The person making the order is called the maker of the note.

Q. What is the difference between an endorsement in blank and a special endorsement ?

(a) By 41 Vict. c. 13 (16th April, 1878), if only the *signature* of the drawee be written on such bill it will be a sufficient acceptance.

A. Bills or notes payable to A. B. or order are transferable by a written order endorsed thereon by A. B. The mere signature by A. B. of his name on the back, followed by the delivery of the bill or note, is, however, sufficient for this purpose. This is called an endorsement in blank, and the bill or note, together with the right to sue upon it, may be transferred by mere delivery. Any holder of a bill may consequently, after such an endorsement, enforce payment to himself. The endorsement may, however, be special, as, "Pay C. D. or order,—A. B.;" and in this case the bill or note, in order to become transferable, must be endorsed by C. D. But if a bill be once endorsed in blank it will always be payable to the bearer by any of the parties thereto, although it may be subsequently specially endorsed.

Q. What is the effect of the Crossed Cheques Act, 1876?

A. This Act contains some very important provisions as to the effect of crossed cheques, as to the effect of general and special crossing, and for the protection of bankers and drawers. (*Vide* the Act, 39 & 40 Vict. c. 81.)

Q. What liability is incurred by accepting a bill or making a promissory note?

A. The effect of accepting a bill or making a promissory note is to render the acceptor or maker primarily liable to pay the same to the person entitled to require payment.

Q. And what is the liability of the drawer, also of any endorser?

A. The effect of drawing a bill is to make the drawer

liable to payment if acceptor makes default. The effect of endorsing a bill or note is to make the endorser also liable to payment if the acceptor of the bill or maker of the note should make default. The endorsement operates as against the endorser as a new drawing of the bill by him. An endorsement may, however, be made without recourse to the endorser, in which case the endorser avoids all personal liability. The drawer of a bill or the endorser of a bill or note will, however, be discharged from all liability unless the person requiring payment should within a reasonable time give him notice that the bill or note has not been paid, or, as it is termed, has been dishonored, and give him to understand, either expressly or by implication, that he looks to him for payment.

Q. Who may enforce payment of a bill or note?

A. A *bonâ fide* holder for valuable consideration or any endorser from him may enforce payment, being entitled to rely on the legal presumption of a proper consideration having been given. By the Bills of Exchange Act, 1871 (34 & 35 Vict. c. 74), bills and notes payable at sight or on presentation are now deemed for all purposes whatsoever to be payable on demand.

Q. In what important particular do special contracts or contracts by deed differ from mere simple contracts?

A. Special contracts or contracts by deed differ from mere simple contracts in the important particular that they of themselves import a consideration, whilst in simple contracts a consideration must be proved.

Q. Can a contract be avoided on the ground of illegality?

A. The object for which a contract is made may be either lawful or unlawful; and if unlawful the contract will be void, and the illegality may be pleaded as a defence to an action brought upon such contract.

Q. Supposing some objects of a contract to be good and others unlawful, will this fact necessarily render the whole contract void?

A. In such case the unlawful objects will not vitiate the others, provided the good part be separable from, and not dependent upon, that which is bad; but if there is any *enactment* to the effect that all instruments containing any matter contrary thereto shall be void, of course everything connected with any instrument containing such matter will be vitiated.

Q. Is a contract in restraint of trade void?

A. Any contract whereby a person is attempted to be restrained from following his usual calling, even for a limited time, is absolutely void. But not so in case of a contract whereby a person is restrained from trading in a particular place, or within a reasonable distance thereof, or from serving a particular class of customers. The rule that contracts in restraint of trade are void at law has been in some respects relaxed in favor of trades unions by the Trades Unions Act, 1871 (amended by 39 & 40 Vict. c. 22; and see 38 & 39 Vict. c. 86).

Q. Define maintenance and champerty.

A. Maintenance, which is the unlawful maintaining of another person's suit, and champerty, which is the maintenance of a suit in consideration of a share in the property to be gained, are both unlawful at common law and by divers ancient statutes. Any contract which commits either of these offences is void.

Q. State some instances in which contracts may be void in consequence of their contravening some Acts of Parliament.

A. Such instances are very numerous; as, for instance, in the case of contracts by clergymen holding benefices, made for the purpose of charging such benefices with any sum of money, which contracts are void under 13 Eliz. c. 20. All contracts or agreements, whether by parol or writing, by way of gaming or wagering, are void; also the contracts of infants (except for necessaries). But the contract of a man too drunk to know what he is about is voidable only, and not void.

Q. What alteration has been effected by the Attorneys and Solicitors Act, 1870, with regard to contracts made by attorneys and solicitors with their clients?

A. Under this Act (33 & 34 Vict. c. 28) an attorney or solicitor may now make an agreement in writing with his client (which before he was not allowed to do) respecting the amount and manner of payment for the whole or any part of any past or future services, fees, charges or disbursements in respect of business done or to be done by him. But such agreements are subject to many provisions and conditions contained in the Act, and intended to be for the security of the client. By the Supreme Court of Judicature Act, 1873, all solicitors, attorneys and proctors are now called solicitors.

CHAPTER III.

OF DEBTS.

Q. What is a debt of record, and what is a court of record?

A. A debt of record is a debt due by the evidence of a court of record. Every court, by having power given to it to fine and imprison, is thereby made a court of record.

Q. What courts are now merged in the Supreme Court of Judicature?

A. By the Judicature Act, 1873, the following superior courts of record, viz., the Courts of Chancery, Queen's Bench, Common Pleas and Exchequer, and the Court of Probate, Divorce and Admiralty. The Supreme Court consists of two permanent divisions, called Her Majesty's High Court of Justice and Her Majesty's Court of Appeal. The High Court of Justice is a superior court of record, and it has had transferred to it the jurisdiction of all the above-mentioned courts, and also of the Court of Common Pleas at Lancaster and the Court of Pleas at Durham. The Court of Appeal is also a superior court of record. The appellate jurisdiction of the House of Lords is now governed by the Appellate Jurisdiction Act, 1876.

Q. What are the inferior courts of record?

A. The inferior courts of record may be said, generally, to consist of the numerous courts established throughout the country under the Acts for the more easy recovery of small debts and demands in England, now called the County Courts Acts.

Q. In the case of debts of record, what creditor has a claim paramount to all others?

A. The crown.

Q. What alteration has been effected as to the distinction between specialty and simple contract debts by the statutes 32 & 33 Vict. c. 46, and 38 & 39 Vict. c. 77, s. 10?

A. By these Acts all specialty debts are reduced to the level of debts by simple contract.

Q. What is a judgment debt?

A. A debt which is due by the *judgment* of a court of record. And as such a debt is due by the evidence of a court of record, it is, of course, a debt of record.

Q. What are now the requisites for the due execution and attestation of warrants of attorney and cognovits?

A. A warrant of attorney to confess judgment in any personal action, or *cognovit actionem*, given by any person, will not be of any force unless there is present a solicitor of the Supreme Court on behalf of such person, expressly named by him and attending at his request, to inform him of the nature and effect of such warrant or cognovit, before the same is executed, who must subscribe his name as a witness to the due execution thereof, and declare that he subscribes as such solicitor. Since the Acts for registering writs of execution warrants of attorney have become almost obsolete.

Q. What is the provision as to the filing of warrants of attorney, cognovits and judge's orders?

A. All warrants of attorney with the defeasances thereto, and all cognovits and all judge's orders or copies thereof, must be filed in the Queen's Bench Division of the High Court, within twenty-one days after their execution, otherwise they will be fraudulent and void.

Q. Do judgment debts carry interest?

A. Every judgment debt carries interest at the rate of 4*l. per cent. per annum*, from the time of entering up such judgment until the same shall be satisfied, and such interest may be levied under a writ of execution on such judgment.

Q. What alteration has been effected by the Supreme Court of Judicature Act, 1875, as to the preference of judgment debts in administration?

A. In the administration by the court of the assets of any person dying after the commencement of that Act, and whose estate may prove to be insufficient for the payment in full of his debts and liabilities, the same rule shall prevail as to the respective rights of secured and unsecured creditors, and as to debts and liabilities provable, as may be in force under the law of bankruptcy with respect to the estates of persons adjudged bankrupt.

Q. What is the effect of the Debtors Act, 1869 (32 & 33 Vict. c. 62) as to imprisonment for debt?

A. It provides that, with the exceptions therein mentioned, no person shall be arrested or imprisoned for default in payment of a sum of money. These exceptions are,

1. Default in payment of a .penalty or sum in the

nature of a penalty other than a penalty in respect of any contract.

2. Default in payment of any sum recoverable summarily before a justice or justices of the peace.

3. Default by a trustee or person acting in a fiduciary capacity, and ordered by a court of equity to pay any sum in his possession or under his control.

4. Default by an attorney or solicitor in payment of costs when ordered to pay costs for misconduct as such, or in payment of a sum of money when ordered to pay the same in his character of an officer of the court making the order.

5. Default in payment for the benefit of creditors of any portion of a salary or other income in respect of the payment of which any court having jurisdiction in bankruptcy is authorized to make an order.

6. Default in payment of sums in respect of the payment of which orders are in that Act authorized to be made.

Q. Describe the two· kinds of *specialty debts*, and whether they now have any, and what, priority over simple contract debts.

A. Specialty debts, or debts secured by *special contract* contained in a deed, are of two kinds, debts by specialty in which the heirs of the debtors are bound, and debts by specialty in which the heirs are not bound; and these formerly took precedence of simple contract debts; but by 32 & 33 Vict. c. 46, 1869, the priority of specialty debts was abolished.

Q. In the case of a bond with a penalty can the obligee recover, either at law or in equity, more than the amount of the penalty?

A. No; but if there be special circumstances in the creditor's favor, as, if he have a mortgage also for the principal and interest, or if the debtor has been delaying him by vexatious proceedings, equity will then aid him to the full extent of his demand.

Q. State the nature of the alterations effected by the Judicature Act, 1873, on all legal proceedings.

A. This Act has abolished the control which equity in many cases formerly exercised over proceedings at law. All legal proceedings are now called actions, and are commenced by a writ of summons, followed when necessary by a statement of plaintiff's claim, to be made within six weeks from the time of defendant's entering his appearance. In every action, law and equity are administered concurrently, but where not otherwise altered all the old forms and rules continue in use.

Q. What are simple contract debts?

A. All debts not secured by the evidence of a court of record, or by deed or specialty. As above shown, they are now payable, *pari passu*, with debts secured by specialty.

Q. On what debts is interest payable?

A. By stat. 3 & 4 Will. 4, c. 42, interest is recoverable on all debts payable by virtue of any written instrument, at a certain time, from the time when such debts were payable, or if payable otherwise, then from the time when demand of payment shall be made in writing, so as such demand give notice to the debtor that interest will be claimed from the date of such demand until the time of payment.

Q. What are the functions and liabilities of sureties?

A. A surety is one who makes himself liable, together with the principal debtor, for the payment of a debt. If he pays the debt he becomes the creditor of the principal debtor for the amount. Every surety who pays a debt is now entitled, by stat. 19 & 20 Vict. c. 97, to have assigned to him every judgment, specialty or other security which shall be held by the creditor in respect of such debt; and, in case of co-sureties, any one surety paying the debt is entitled to contribution from his co-sureties in equal shares; or if they should have been sureties to unequal amounts, then in proportion to the respective amounts to which they have made themselves liable.

Q. How may a surety be discharged from his liability?

A. By the conduct of the creditor. As surety, he has made himself liable only for the payment of a particular debt, at a given time, or under certain circumstances. If, therefore, the creditor, by any subsequent arrangement with the principal debtor, preclude himself from demanding payment of his debt at the time or under the circumstances originally agreed on, the surety will at once be discharged from all liability. Thus, if the creditor bind himself to give further time for payment to the principal debtor, or compound with him, without expressly reserving his remedy against the surety, the surety will be discharged.

Q. How were debts formerly assigned at law?

A. An authority from the creditor to the assignee to sue the debtor in the creditor's name was given. This was called a power of attorney, and was not required

4*

to be by deed, but might have been by writing unsealed, or even by parol.

Q. In the event of bankruptcy since the Act of 1869, how may the trustees of a bankrupt sue and be sued, and how may the debts be recovered?

A. The trustee may sue by the official name of "The trustee of the property of A. B., a bankrupt." And any person to whom anything in action belonging to the bankrupt is assigned, in pursuance of that Act, may bring or defend any action or suit relating to such thing in action in his own name.

Q. State the general rule as to the payment of debts.

A. In the first place, the payment of a smaller sum is no satisfaction of a larger one, unless there be some consideration for the relinquishment of the residue, such as the payment at an earlier time than the whole is due, or the concurrence of some or all of the other creditors of the debtor in accepting a composition. But it seems that the acceptance of a negotiable security for a small amount may be a good satisfaction for a larger debt, and the payment of a small sum may be a good satisfaction for an unliquidated demand for large pecuniary damages on account of the uncertainty of such a claim.

Q. What is the rule as to the appropriation of payments?

A. When a less sum is paid to the creditor than the whole amount of his demands it is competent to the debtor to make the payment in satisfaction of any demand he may please; but if made generally the creditor may elect at the time of payment, or within a reasonable time after, to appropriate the money to whichever demand he may please. And if no election be made on either side the law will, in ordinary cases of current accounts, presume that the first item on the debit side is discharged or reduced by the first payment entered on the credit side, and so on in the order of time. Interest, when any due, being payable in the first place, then principal *pro tanto*.

Q. How are compositions with creditors now effected?

A. Under the 125th and 126th sections of the Bankruptcy Act, 1869.

Q. What is the effect of the regulations as to liquidation by arrangement made by the Bankruptcy Act, 1869?

A. The debtor presents a petition to the proper court, with affidavits annexed, according to the forms in the Schedule to the Rules (Nos. 106 and 107), and a general meeting of his creditors is summoned by the registrar on a day within one calendar month from the presentation of the petition, when they may by special resolution declare that the affairs of the debtor are to be liquidated by arrangement and not in bankruptcy, and may at that or some subsequent meeting, held not more than a week off, appoint a trustee with or without a committee of inspection. This special resolution, together with the statement of the assets and debts of a debtor, and the name of the trustee appointed and of the members (if any) of the committee of inspection, is presented to the registrar and registered by him; and the liquidation is deemed to commence from the date of the appointment of the trustee. All such property of the debtor as would, if he were made bankrupt, be di-

visible amongst his creditors is vested in the trustee,
and all deeds and proceedings, &c., as would be void in
case of bankruptcy are void as against the trustee,
who has the same power as the trustee in bankruptcy,
and the property is distributable in like manner. The
close of the liquidation may be fixed; the discharge of
the debtor and the release of the trustee may be
granted by a special resolution of the creditors in general meeting, and the accounts may be audited, in pursuance of such resolution, at such time and in such
manner and upon such terms and conditions as the creditors think fit. The trustee reports to the registrar the
discharge of the debtor, and a certificate of such discharge given by the registrar has the same effect as an
order of discharge under the Act.

Q. What is the difference between liquidation by arrangement and composition?

A. Liquidation is thus explained by the present
chief judge in bankruptcy: "Liquidation may be said,
in general terms, to be an equivalent for bankruptcy,
giving the creditors the same rights which they have in
bankruptcy. But composition is a totally different
thing. All that the law requires from a debtor propos-
ing to compound with his creditors is that he should
state fully what his means are of paying his debts,
having first stated truly what is the amount of those
debts. And if the creditors agree to accept his composition he becomes a free man, entitled to all the
rights of ownership and disposition over every part of
his property. The creditors relinquish the rights which
the law would give them if they proceed to bankruptcy

or liquidation by arrangement, and they are content that the debtor should thenceforth deal with his property in any way he thinks fit."

Q. What provision is made by the Bankruptcy Act, 1869 (sect. 126), for a debtor effecting a composition with his creditors?

A. "The creditors of a debtor unable to pay his debts may, without any proceedings in bankruptcy, by an extraordinary resolution, resolve that a composition shall be accepted in satisfaction of the debts due to them from the debtor."

Q. What is an extraordinary resolution?

A. An extraordinary resolution is one passed by a majority in number and three-fourths in value of the creditors at a general meeting, summoned as required by Rules 254 and 259, and confirmed by a majority in number and value of the creditors assembled at a subsequent general meeting (of which notice has been given as required by Rule 282) held not less than seven days nor more than fourteen days from the first meeting.

Q. How are proceedings for liquidation and composition commenced, and what advantage has a secured creditor over ordinary creditors?

A. They are commenced by petition, with an affidavit thereto annexed according to prescribed forms. The petition must be addressed to the court to which a bankruptcy petition against the debtor could be presented. A secured creditor, unless he shall have realized his security, shall, previously to being allowed to prove or vote, state in his proof the particulars of his security and the value at which he assesses to same; and he shall be deemed to be a creditor only in respect of the balance due to him after deducting such assessed value of the security.

Q. Where will the terms of composition appear?

A. The extraordinary resolution may provide that the terms be embodied in a deed containing covenants for securing the composition and releasing the debtor, as may be specified in the resolution. (Rule 281.)

Q. What is the effect of a failure of a debtor to comply with the provisions of a composition?

A. The creditors will no longer be restrained from proceeding to enforce the full payment of their debts.

CHAPTER IV.

OF BANKRUPTCY OF TRADERS.

Q. Who are traders?

A. The 4th section of the Act enacts, by reference to the schedule to the Act, that all alum makers, apothecaries, auctioneers, bankers, bleachers, brokers, brickmakers, builders, calenderers, carpenters, carriers, cattle or sheep salesmen, coach proprietors, cowkeepers, dyers, fullers, keepers of inns, taverns, hotels, coffeehouses, lime-burners, livery stable-keepers, market gardeners, millers, packers, printers, sharebrokers, shipowners, shipwrights, stock brokers, stock jobbers, victuallers, warehousemen, wharfingers, persons using the trade or profession of a scrivener, receiving other men's money or estates into their trusts or custody, persons insuring ships or their freight or other matters against perils of the sea, persons using the trade or merchandise, by way of bargaining, exchange, bartering, commission, consignment or otherwise, in gross or by retail; and persons who, either for themselves or as agents or factors for others, seek their living by buying and selling or by buying and letting for hire, or by the workmanship or the conversion of goods or commodities, are traders.

Q. Who are not traders?

A. The schedule provides that "a farmer, grazier, common laborer, or workman for hire, shall not, nor shall a member of any partnership, association or company which cannot be adjudged bankrupt under the Act, be deemed as such a trader for any purposes of this Act."

Q. Name the acts of bankruptcy.

A. 1. That the debtor has in England or elsewhere made a conveyance or assignment of his property to a trustee or trustees for the benefit of his creditors generally.

2. That the debtor has in England or elsewhere made a fraudulent conveyance, gift, delivery or transfer of his property or any part thereof.

3. That the debtor has, with intent to defeat or delay his creditors, done any of the following things, namely, departed out of England, or being out of England remained out of England, or being a trader departed from his dwelling-house or otherwise absented himself, or begun to keep house, or suffered himself to be outlawed.

4. That the debtor has filed in the prescribed manner in the court a declaration admitting his inability to pay his debts.

5. That the execution issued against the debtor on any legal process for the purpose of obtaining payment of not less than fifty pounds has in the case of a trader been levied by seizure and sale of his goods.

6. That the creditor presenting the petition has served in the prescribed manner on the debtor a debtor's summons requiring the debtor to pay a sum due, of an amount of not less than fifty pounds; and the debtor, being a trader, has for the space of seven days, or not being a trader, has for the space of three weeks succeeding the service of such summons, neglected to pay such sum or to secure or compound for the same.

Q. What is a fraudulent conveyance?

A. A fraudulent conveyance sometimes resolves itself into the question of the debtor's intention in making the conveyance, and sometimes is concluded from the nature of the conveyance itself. A *bonâ fide* intent to carry on his business and to procure advances for that purpose will sustain a mortgage of the whole or nearly all of the debtor's property.

Q. When can a debtor be arrested under the Absconding Debtors Act, 1870?

A. The Absconding Debtors Act, 1870, empowers the Court of Bankruptcy to arrest any debtor who has been served with a debtor's summons, if there be probable reason for believing that he is about to go abroad with a view of avoiding payment of the debt, or of avoiding service of a petition of bankruptcy, or of avoiding appearing to such petition, or of avoiding examination in respect of his affairs, or otherwise avoiding, delaying or embarrassing proceedings in bankruptcy.

Q. State the requisites to support a petition for adjudication in bankruptcy.

A. The requisites are, a sufficient petitioning creditor's debt or debts, which must amount to not less than 50*l.* ; and the trading must be proved where necessary ; and an act of bankruptcy within six calendar months. (Sect. 8.)

Q. Must the adjudication be advertised? and how?

A. Yes; the adjudication must be published in the London Gazette, and be advertised locally in such manner (if any) as may be described, and the date of such order shall be the date of the adjudication for the purposes of the Act, and the production of a copy of the Gazette, containing such order as aforesaid, shall be conclusive evidence.

Q. In whom does the bankrupt's property now vest upon adjudication ?

A. In the registrar, who acts as trustee until one is appointed, when it vests in the latter.

Q. State the chief matters to be resolved upon at the first meeting of creditors.

A. 1. To appoint a trustee.

2. To declare if any, and what, security is to be given, and to whom, by the person so appointed.

3. To appoint a committee of inspection if desired, not exceeding five in number, to superintend the administration of the bankrupt's property.

4. The creditors *may* also give directions as to the

manner in which the property is to be administered by the trustee.

Q. What property does not vest in the trustee?

A. 1. Property held in trust for any other person.

2. The tools of his trade and necessary wearing apparel and bedding of himself, wife and children to the extent of 20*l*. (Sect. 15.)

Q. What property may the trustee disclaim?

A. The trustee may disclaim land of any tenure burdened with onerous covenants, or unmarketable shares in companies, or unprofitable contracts, or any other property that is unsalable or not readily salable by reason of its binding the possessor thereof to the performance of any onerous act or to the payment of any sum of money.

Q. What property vests in the trustee?

A. All property which belonged to or vested in the bankrupt at the commencement of the bankruptcy, or which is acquired by or devolves on him during its continuance; all powers which the bankrupt might exercise for his own benefit except the nomination to a vacant ecclesiastical benefice; and the goods and chattels at the commencement of the bankruptcy in the possession, order or disposition of the bankrupt, being a trader, with the consent and permission of the true owner, of which the bankrupt is reputed owner, or has undertaken the sale or disposition as owner; but things in action, other than debts due in course of trade or business, are excepted.

Q. What power has the trustee?

A. By sect. 25, subject to the provisions of the Act, the trustee has power to do the following things:—

1. To receive and decide upon proofs of debts, and for such purposes to administer oaths.

2. To carry on the business of the bankrupt, as far as may be necessary for the beneficial winding up of the same.

3. To bring or defend any action, suit or other legal proceeding relating to the property of the bankrupt.

4. To deal with any property to which the bankrupt is beneficially entitled as tenant in tail, in the same manner as the bankrupt might have dealt with the same. (Sects. 56 to 73 of 3 & 4 Will. 4, c. 74, to extend and apply to proceedings under this Act.)

5. To exercise any powers, the capacity to exercise which is vested in him under this Act, and to exercise all powers of attorney, deeds and other instruments expedient or necessary.

6. To sell all the property of the bankrupt (including the goodwill of the business, if any, and the book debts due or growing due to the bankrupt), by public auction (see Rule 119) or private contract, with power, if he thinks fit, to transfer the whole to any person or company, or to sell the same in parcels.

7. To give receipts, which shall effectually discharge the person paying.

8. To prove rank, claim and draw a dividend in the matter of the bankruptcy or sequestration of any debtor of the bankrupt; and to appoint the bankrupt himself to superintend the management of the property or of any part thereof, or to carry on his trade for the benefit of the creditors. (Sects. 25, 26.)

Q. And what are his powers with the sanction of the committee of inspection?

A. 1. He may mortgage or pledge any part of the property of the bankrupt for the purpose of raising money for the payment of his debts.

2. Refer any dispute to arbitration, compromise all debts, claims and liabilities whatever upon such terms as may be agreed upon.

3. Compromise with creditors in respect of any debts provable under the bankruptcy.

4. Compromise any claim arising out of or incidental to the property of the bankrupt.

5. Divide in its existing form amongst the creditors, according to its estimated value, any property which cannot advantageously be realized by sale.

The sanction given for the purposes of this section may be a general permission to do all or any of the above-mentioned things, or a permission to do all or any of them in any specified case or cases. (Sect. 27.)

Q. When traders' goods are seized in execution by the sheriff, who is entitled to the proceeds?

A. Execution levied by seizure and sale of the goods of any trader debtor for the recovery of a debt exceeding 50l. is now an act of bankruptcy, and the sheriff or officer of the County Court shall retain the proceeds of such sale in his hands for fourteen days, and on notice of petition presented, shall hold the proceeds, after deducting the expenses in trust for the trustee; but if no such notice be served, or the trader is not adjudged bankrupt on such petition, or any other of which he may have notice, he may pay over proceeds to execution creditor. (Sect. 87.)

Q. What description of debts are now provable in bankruptcy?

A. All debts and liabilities, present or future, certain or contingent, to which the bankrupt is subject at the date of the order of adjudication, or to which he may become subject during the continuance of the bankruptcy, by reason of any obligation incurred previously to the date of the order of adjudication. (Sect. 31.)

Q. What is included under the head of liability?

A. Any compensation for work or labor done, any obligation or possibility thereof to pay money or money's worth on the breach of any express or implied covenant, contract, agreement or undertaking, whether capable of accruing or not, before the close of the bankruptcy, and whether such payment be fixed or unliquidated in amount, or dependent on contingencies, or can be valued by fixed rules or only by a jury, or as a matter of opinion. (Sect. 31.)

Q. What is the extent of a landlord's remedy against the estate of a bankrupt for rent, or a proportionate part of rent?

A. A distress for rent levied after the commencement of the bankruptcy is available for only one year's rent accrued prior to the date of the order of adjudication, but the landlord may prove for an overplus of rent due. (Sect. 34.) If the adjudication is made between two days of payment of rent, the person entitled may prove for a proportionate part to the date of adjudication. (Sect. 35.)

Q. Can any, and what, allowance be made to the bankrupt for maintenance or services ?

A. The trustee, with the consent of the creditors, testified by a resolution passed in general meeting, may from time to time make such allowance as may be approved by the creditors out of the property for the support of the bankrupt and his family, or in consideration of his services if he is engaged in winding up his estate. (Sect. 38.)

Q. In what cases will a set-off be allowed in bankruptcy ?

A. Where there have been mutual credits, debts or dealings between the bankrupt and any other person claiming to prove under the bankruptcy an account shall be taken of what is due in respect thereof, and the balance only shall be claimed or paid, provided that the person claiming the benefit of such set-off had not when such credit was given notice of any act of bankruptcy by such bankrupt committed and available against him for adjudication. (Sect. 39.)

Q. What is the effect of the provision in sect. 40 of the Act as to secured creditors ?

A. He can, on giving up his security, prove for the whole debt, or he may prove for the balance after realizing his security or giving credit for the value of it (sect. 40) ; in the latter case he gives notice to the trustee, who, or any creditor, may call upon him to realize if dissatisfied with the value put upon it. (Rule 136.)

Q. What are the present provisions under the Act of 1869 as regards the protection of certain transactions entered into with bankrupts ?

A. The following are protected :—1. Any disposition or contract with respect to the disposition of property by conveyance, transfer, charge, delivery, payment or otherwise, made in good faith and for value.

2. Any execution or attachment against land executed by seizure; or,

3. Against the goods if executed by seizure and sale. (Sect. 95.)

Q. In what cases, and within what time, may voluntary settlements be avoided under the Bankruptcy Act, 1869?

A. Any settlement of property made by a trader, not being for value, or of the wife's property, will, if the settlor becomes bankrupt within *two years* after the date of such settlement, be void as against the trustee of the bankrupt appointed under the Act, and will, if the settlor becomes bankrupt at any subsequent time within ten years after the date of such settlement, unless the parties claiming under such settlement can prove that the settlor was at the time of making the settlement able to pay all his debts without the aid of the property comprised in such settlement, be void against such trustee.

Q. Are conveyances or transfers of property voidable on account of fraudulent preference, and in what cases?

A. Such conveyances are void if the maker become bankrupt within *three months* of the date thereof, as against the trustee of the bankrupt appointed under this Act; but this does not affect the rights of a purchaser, payee or incumbrancer, in good faith and for valuable consideration.

Q. What rent may the landlord of a bankrupt dis-

train for, and what other claims also take a priority
under the Bankruptcy Acts?

A. The landlord may distrain for his rent not exceeding one year's rent accrued prior to the day of the
filing of the petition for adjudication. The court may
order to be paid in full : four months' wages or salary
of a clerk or servant, not exceeding 50*l.* ; and the wages
of any laborer or workman, not exceeding two months.
Priority is also given to parochial and other rates and
all assessed taxes, land tax and property or income tax,
assessed on the debtor up to the 5th of April next before
the order of adjudication, and not exceeding one year's
assessment.

Q. What are the present provisions under the Bankruptcy Act, 1869, with respect to the *order of discharge ?*

A. When a bankruptcy is closed or at any time during
its continuance, with the assent of the creditors, testified
by a special resolution, the bankrupt may apply for an
order of discharge ; but such discharge shall not be
granted unless it is proved to the court that one of the
following conditions has been fulfilled, that is to say,
either that a dividend of not less than ten shillings in
the pound has been paid out of his property, or might
have been paid except through the negligence or fraud
of the trustee, or that a special resolution of his creditors has been passed to the effect that his bankruptcy
or his failure to pay ten shillings in the pound has, in
their opinion, arisen from circumstances for which the
bankrupt cannot justly be held responsible, and they
desire that an order of discharge should be granted him,

but the court may suspend or withhold the same if a bankrupt has made default in giving up to his creditors any property, or a prosecution has been commenced against him under the Fraudulent Debtors Act, 1869.

Q. What is the effect of such order?

A. It does not release the bankrupt from any debt or liability incurred by means of any fraud or breach of trust, nor from any debt or liability whereof he has obtained forbearance by any fraud; but it releases the bankrupt from all other debts provable under bankruptcy with the exception of—

1. Debts due to the crown;

2. Debts with which the bankrupt stands charged at the suit of the crown or under the revenue laws, or on a bail bond to appear thereto.

Q. And what are the provisions of that Act with regard to the status of an undischarged bankrupt?

A. 1. No portion of a debt provable under the bankruptcy can be enforced against his property for three years from the close of the bankruptcy; and during that time, if he makes up the dividend to his creditors ten shillings in the pound, he may apply for his order of discharge.

2. At the expiration of three years, if he has not obtained an order of discharge, any balance remaining unpaid in respect of any debt proved in such bankruptcy (but without interest in the meantime) shall be deemed to be a subsisting debt in the nature of a judgment debt, which, subject to the rights of any persons who have become creditors of the debtor since the close of his bankruptcy, may be enforced against any prop-

erty of the debtor with the sanction of the court which adjudicated such debtor a bankrupt, or of the court having jurisdiction in bankruptcy in the place where the property is situated, but to the extent only, and at the time and manner, directed by such court, and after giving such notice and doing such acts as may be prescribed in that behalf.

Q. What is the effect of the Act of 1869 as respects persons having privilege of Parliament?

A. They may now be dealt with under the Act of 1869 in like manner as if they had not such privilege; and if a member of the House of Commons is adjudged bankrupt he is to remain for one year from the date of the order of adjudication incapable of sitting and voting in the House unless within that time either the order is annulled or the creditors who prove the debts under the bankruptcy are fully paid and satisfied.

CHAPTER V.

OF BANKRUPTCY OF NON-TRADERS.

Q. What alteration was made by the Bankruptcy Act, 1861, with respect to the insolvency of persons not in trade?

A. By the Bankruptcy Act, 1861, all persons, whether traders or not, became subject to the bankruptcy law; but no person was to be adjudged a bank-

rupt except in respect of some one of the acts of
bankruptcy described in the Act as applicable to non-
traders.

Q. What is the law as to the sequestration of a clergyman's benefice?

A. Where a bankrupt is a beneficed clergyman, the
trustee may apply for a sequestration of the profits of
the benefice, and the certificate of the appointment of
the trustee will be sufficient authority for the granting
of sequestration without any writ or other proceeding.

Q. Also when a bankrupt is an officer in the army
or navy?

A. Where a bankrupt is or has been an officer of the
army or navy, in the civil service of the crown, or is in
the enjoyment of any pension or compensation granted
by the treasury, the trustee during the bankruptcy, and
the registrar after the close of the bankruptcy, may
receive for distribution amongst the creditors so much
of the bankrupt's pay, half-pay, salary, emolument or
pension as the court, upon the application of the trustee,
thinks just and reasonable, to be paid in such manner
and at such times as the court, with the consent in
writing of the chief officer of the department under
which the pay, half-pay, salary, emolument, pension or
compensation is enjoyed, directs.

Q. Where a bankrupt is in receipt of a salary, can
the court make an order for appropriation?

A. The court, upon the application of the trustee,
shall from time to time make such order as it thinks
just for the payment of such salary or income, or of
any part thereof, to the trustee during the bankruptcy,

and to the registrar, if necessary, after the close of the bankruptcy, to be applied by him in such manner as the court may direct.

CHAPTER VI.

OF INSURANCE.

Q. What is a policy of insurance, and what are the most usual kinds of insurance?

A. It is an instrument by which a contract to insure is entered into; and a contract to insure is a contract either to indemnify against a loss which may arise on the happening of some event, or to pay, on the happening of some event, a sum of money to the person insured. The most usual kinds of insurance are, insurance of *lives*, insurance against loss or damage by *fire*, and insurance of *ships* and their cargoes.

Q. What is the effect of an insurance where the insurer has no interest in the person whose life is insured?

A. It is enacted by 14 Geo. 3, c. 48, that no insurance shall be made on the life of any person, or on any other event whatsoever, wherein the person for whose use and benefit or on whose account such policy shall be made shall have no interest, or by way of gaming or wagering; and that every such assurance shall be null and void.

Q. May a person insure his own life? and in what case will such an insurance become void?

A. Any person may insure his own life, but if he should afterwards commit suicide, or die by sentence of the law (or in a duel), the insurance will be void in the hands of his executors. But in the above cases, supposing the policy to have been previously assigned, it will not be void as against an assignee.

Q. Has a creditor an insurable interest in the life of his debtor, and to what extent?

A. He has, to the extent of his debt; and by recent decisions the doctrine that a life insurance was a contract for indemnity only has been overruled; so that, if the person insuring has an insurable interest at the time of effecting the policy, the subsequent loss of such interest will not render the policy void.(*a*)

Q. Has a trustee such an interest as is sufficient to support a life insurance?

A. An interest as trustee is sufficient to support a life insurance. But a father has not such an interest in the life of his child as to warrant an insurance of it for his own benefit.(*b*)

Q. In case a life policy is assigned, is notice of such assignment required to be given to the insurance company? and if no such notice be given, what will be the consequence?

A. Since the passing of the Act 30 & 31 Vict. c. 144, no assignment of a policy of life assurance will

---

(*a*) *Dalby* v. *India and London Life Assurance Co.*, C. B. 365; S. C. 18 *Jur.* 1024; *Law* v. *London Indisputable Life Policy Co.*, 1 Kay & John. 223.

(*b*) *Halford* v. *Kymer*, 10 Barn. & Cress. 724; *Worthington* v. *Curtis*, C. A. L. R., 1 Ch. D. 419.

confer on the assignee therein named, his executors, administrators or assigns, any right to sue on such policy until a written notice of such assignment be given to the assurance company at their principal place of business.

Q. What are the provisions of the Married Women's Property Act, 1870, with respect to policies of life assurance?

A. A married woman may effect a policy of assurance upon her own life or the life of her husband for her separate use; and if so expressed on the face of the policy, all benefit therefrom shall enure accordingly, and the contract be as valid as if made with an unmarried woman.

Q. Is it necessary that a person who effects a fire insurance shall have an interest in the property insured? and to what extent can he insure?

A. The person who effects such insurance must have an interest in the property insured, and he cannot recover beyond the extent of his interest; neither can he assign his policy without the consent of the insurers. When the building is within the limits of the Metropolitan Building Acts, any person interested may procure the insurance money in case of fire, to be laid out in repairs or rebuilding.

Q. Under the Metropolitan Building Acts, what is the effect of a covenant to insure against fire?

A. A covenant to insure any building within such limits is tantamount to a covenant to repair to the extent of such insurance, and if entered into by a lessee in his lease will *run with the land*, so as to be binding on the assignee of the lease; and it has been recently decided that the law is the same even if the building be situate beyond the above-mentioned limits.(a)

Q. What is the effect of the statute 22 & 23 Vict. c. 35, s. 7, as to relief against the forfeiture for breach of a covenant to insure against fire?

A. This enactment empowers a court of equity to relieve against a forfeiture for breach of a covenant to insure against fire when no loss or damage by fire has happened, and the breach has, in the opinion of the court, been committed through accident or mistake, or otherwise, without fraud or gross negligence, and there is an insurance on foot at the time of the application to the court in conformity with the covenant to insure; but the same person can only be relieved once, and not then if a former breach has been waived.

Q. What is the effect of the statute 31 & 32 Vict. c. 86, s. 1, as regards an assignee of a marine policy?

A. Wherever a policy of insurance on any ship, or any goods in any ship, or in any freight, has been assigned so as to pass the beneficial interest in such policy to any person entitled to the property thereby insured, the assignee of such policy shall be entitled to sue thereon in his own name.

Q. What is bottomry?

A. Bottomry is an agreement by which a vessel is hypothecated or pledged by the owner for the payment, in the event of her voyage terminating successfully, of money advanced to him for the necessary use of the

(a) 4 Jur., N. S., Pt. 2, p. 132; *Simpson* v. *Scottish Union, &c.*, V.-C. W. 11 W. R. 459, and other cases.

vessel, together with interest, which interest, in consideration of the risk incurred, is generally far beyond 5*l.* per cent.

Q. What is respondentia?

A. Respondentia is a somewhat similar contract with respect to the cargo, except that the borrower only is responsible in the event of the safe termination of the voyage, the lender having no lien on the goods.

CHAPTER VII.

OF ARBITRATION.

Q. What jurisdiction has the High Court of Justice over matters agreed to be referred to arbitration?

A. As the High Court of Justice has full jurisdiction on all questions arising out of agreements of any kind, it follows that it retains a jurisdiction over matters which the parties themselves have agreed should be referred to arbitration. Notwithstanding, therefore, an agreement to refer disputes to arbitration, either party may bring the matter into court. But in such a case, on application, the court may stay proceedings on being satisfied that no just cause exists why it should not be referred to arbitration, and that the defendant was and is ready to concur in all acts necessary to carry out such reference.

Q. What is the provision in the Common Law Procedure Act, 1854, as to ordinary matters of account to be referred to arbitration?

A. By this Act the court has power, upon the application of either party, to order any matter in dispute which consists wholly or in part of matters of mere account to be referred to arbitration upon such terms as to costs and otherwise as the court may think reasonable.

Q. What are official referees under the Supreme Court of Judicature Act, 1873, and what is a special referee?

A. This Act provides for the appointment of permanent officers called official referees; and in any cause or matter (other than a criminal proceeding by the crown) the court or a judge has power, with the consent of all parties interested who are under no disability, and also without such consent in any matter requiring a prolonged examination of documents or accounts, or any scientific or local investigation which cannot conveniently be made before a jury or conducted by the court through its ordinary officers, to order any question or issue of fact or any question of account arising thereon to be tried either before an official referee or before a special referee to be agreed upon between the parties. The report of such referee, unless set aside by the court, is equivalent to the verdict of a jury.

Q. What are the sittings of the courts?

A. The sittings of the Court of Appeal and the sittings in London and Middlesex of the High Court of Justice are four in every year, viz., the Michaelmas sittings, the Hilary sittings, the Easter sittings and the Trinity sittings.

Q. What is the provision of the Common Law Procedure Act, 1854, as to making a submission to arbitration a rule of court?

A. That every agreement or submission to arbitration by consent, whether by deed or in writing, may be made a rule of any of the superior courts of law or equity, unless the contrary is stipulated therein; but a parol submission cannot be made a rule of court, even although made pursuant to an agreement to refer contained in a deed.

Q. What power is given by that Act to a judge to appoint an arbitrator in case the parties do not concur in so doing?

A. Where reference is authorized to be made to a single arbitrator, and all parties do not, after differences have arisen, concur in appointment of an arbitrator, or if an arbitrator dies or refuses or becomes incapable to act, and the terms of the document authorizing the reference do not show that it was intended that such vacancy should not be supplied, and the parties do not concur in appointing a fresh one, then any party may serve the remaining parties with a written notice to appoint an arbitrator, and if within seven clear days after such notice no arbitrator is appointed, a judge of any of the superior courts of law or equity at Westminster, upon summons to be issued by the party who has given such notice, may appoint an arbitrator, who will have the same power to act and make his award as if he had been appointed by consent of all parties.

Q. Within what time must an arbitrator make his award?

A. Where no time is limited, the award must be made within a reasonable time; but if a time is limited,

the award must be made within such time, unless the
time for making it is enlarged. Under a compulsory
order of reference, unless specified to the contrary, it
must be made within three months after entering upon
the reference.

Q. Is the attendance of the parties necessary in arbitration proceedings? and describe shortly the mode of
procedure.

A. The arbitrators are bound to require the attendance of the parties, for which purpose notice of the
meetings should be given them. In taking evidence,
arbitrators may proceed in any way they please if the
parties have due notice of their proceedings and do not
object before the award is made. But each must use
his own judgment, and in order to obviate any objection
they ought to proceed in the admission of evidence according to the ordinary rules of law.

Q. In what cases may an arbitrator state a special
case for the opinion of the court?

A. On any compulsory reference under the Common
Law Procedure Act, 1854, or upon any reference by
consent where the submission is or may be made a rule
of any of the superior courts at Westminster, the arbitrator may if he thinks proper, and if it is not provided
to the contrary, state his award as to the whole or any
part thereof in the form of a special case for the opinion
of the court; and when an action is referred, judgment,
if so ordered, may be entered according to the opinion
of the court.

Q. Within what time must an application be made to
set aside any compulsory award?

A. Within the first seven days of the term next following the publication of the award to the parties, whether made in vacation or term.

Q. How is an umpire appointed, and what is his authority?

A. The Common Law Procedure Act, 1854, provides that when the reference is to two arbitrators, and the terms of the document authorizing it do not show that it was intended that there should *not* be an umpire, or provide otherwise for the appointment of an umpire, the two arbitrators may appoint an umpire any time within the period during which they have power to make an award; and on failure of their so doing, a judge, on summons to be taken out as mentioned in the Act (sect. 12), may appoint an umpire. The authority of an umpire to make an award commences from the time of the disagreement of the arbitrators; he ought to hear the whole evidence over again, unless the parties should be satisfied with his deciding on the statement of the arbitrators. And the whole matter in difference must be submitted to his decision, and not only some particular points on which the arbitrators differ.

Q. Does an award for payment of money create a debt for which an action may be brought, and would it be sufficient to support a petition for adjudication in bankruptcy?

A. It does; but when the award is made a rule of court its performance may be enforced by attachment, and, if necessary, the court will decree a specific performance.

PART III.

OF INCORPOREAL PERSONAL PROPERTY.

CHAPTER I.

OF PERSONAL ANNUITIES, STOCKS AND SHARES.

Q. What description of property is stock in the funds?

A. By various statutes it has been provided that it shall be personal estate, and not descendible to the heir.

Q. How is the transfer of stock in the public funds effected?

A. By the signature of the books at the Bank of England, in the manner prescribed by Act of Parliament; and this may be done either in person or by attorney thereunto lawfully authorized by writing under hand and seal, attested by two or more credible witnesses.

Q. And how when the stock is standing in the name of a trustee?

A. In such case the beneficial owner may transfer his equitable interest in any manner he pleases without any power of attorney; and the transferee, on giving notice of the transfer to the trustee, will be entitled to a legal transfer of the stock into his own name in the books at the bank.

Q. Does a contract for the sale of stock come within the 17th section of the Statute of Frauds?

A. No; stock is not *goods*, *wares* or *merchandise* within that section, so that it does not require a written memorandum for a contract for its sale if the value exceeds 10*l.*, and the buyer does not accept and receive any part, nor give something in earnest to bind the bargain, or in part payment.

Q. What is the nature and effect of a *distringas?*

A. When a person has an interest in stock standing in the name of another, he is enabled to restrain the transfer of such stock, or, as it is said, to put a *stop upon it*, by means of a writ of *distringas*, to be served upon the Bank of England, and which is obtained from the Chancery Division of the High Court.

Q. Has any, and what, alteration been made in the law as to stock being charged with judgment debts?

A. Stock, being a kind of *chose in action*, could not formerly have been sold under a *fieri facias*, issued in execution of a judgment against the owner. The Supreme Court of Judicature Act, 1875, now provides that an order charging stock or shares may be made by any divisional court or by any judge, and the proceedings for obtaining such order shall be such as are directed, and the effect shall be such as is provided, by the several Acts relating thereto.

Q. What is a corporation sole, and what is a corporation aggregate?

A. A corporation *sole* is composed of only one person, such as a bishop, a parson, or the chamberlain of London. A corporation *aggregate* is composed of many persons acting on all solemn occasions by the medium of their *common seal*. They are created either by charter, conferred by the queen's letters patent, or by Act of Parliament.

Q. What description of property are New River shares?

A. Like some of the older companies' shares they are real estate in the nature of incorporeal hereditaments.

Q. What Acts govern the constitution of public companies?

A. The Companies Clauses Consolidation Act, 1845 (8 & 9 Vict. c. 16), the Companies Clauses Act, 1863 (26 & 27 Vict. c. 118), and the Companies Clauses Act, 1869 (32 & 33 Vict. c. 48).

Q. What is the Act which now regulates the management and winding up of all joint stock companies?

A. The Companies Act, 1862 (25 & 26 Vict. c. 89, amended by 30 & 31 Vict. c. 131 and 40 & 41 Vict. c. 26), which has repealed and consolidated all the former Acts relating to joint stock companies.

Q. State the effect of the Companies Acts, 1862 and 1867.

A. Under these Acts seven or more persons associated for any lawful purpose may, by subscribing their names to a memorandum of association, and otherwise complying with the requisitions of the Acts in respect of registration, form an incorporated company, with or without liability.

Q. How far may the liability of the members of a company formed under the Companies Act, 1862, be limited?

A. It may, according to the memorandum of association, be limited either to the amount (if any) unpaid on the shares respectively held by them, or to such amount as the members may respectively undertake, by the memorandum of association, to contribute to the assets of the company in the event of its being wound up. In the former case it is said to be limited "by shares" and in the latter "by guarantee."

Q. What are the requisites of a memorandum of association of a company limited by shares?

A. Such memorandum must contain the following things:

1. The name of the company, with the addition of the word "limited."

2. The part of the United Kingdom where the registered office of the company is proposed to be situate.

3. The objects for which the company is to be established.

4. A declaration that the liability of the members is limited.

5. The amount of capital with which the company proposes to be registered, divided into shares of a certain fixed amount, subject to the following regulations: (1) That no subscriber shall take less than one share; (2) That each subscriber of the memorandum of association shall write opposite to his name the number of shares he takes.

Q. And what in the case of a company limited by guarantee?

A. The memorandum of association must contain the first three of the above-named requisites, and (4) a declaration that each member undertakes to contribute to the assets of the company in the event of the same being wound up during the time that he is a member, or within one year afterwards; for the payment of the debts and liabilities of the company contracted before the time at which he ceases to be a member, and of the costs, charges and expenses of winding up the company; and for the adjustment of the rights of the contributories amongst themselves, such amount as may be required, not exceeding a specified amount.

Q. And what in the case of an unlimited company?

A. The memorandum of association must contain only the following things :—

1. The name of the company.

2. The part of the United Kingdom in which the registered office of the company is proposed to be situate.

3. The objects for which the company is to be established.

Q. Are articles of association necessary both in the case of a company limited by shares and a company limited by guarantee or unlimited?

A. The memorandum of association may in case of a company limited by shares, and must in the case of a company limited by guarantee or unlimited, be accompanied when registered by articles of association, signed by the subscribers to the memorandum of association, and prescribing such regulations for the company as the subscribers shall deem expedient.

Q. When the memorandum and articles (if necessary) are complete, what further is necessary?

A. The memorandum and articles (if any) are to be registered by the registrar of joint stock companies, and thereupon the company is incorporated with power to hold lands ; and a certificate of the incorporation of any company given by the registrar shall be conclusive evidence that all the requisitions of the Act in respect of registration. have been complied with.   Every company is bound by the Act to have a registered office, and every limited company must have its name painted or affixed on the outside of the office or place of business of the company.

Q. When is a resolution passed by a company under the Act deemed to be a special resolution ?

A. A resolution passed by a company under the Act is deemed special whenever a resolution has been passed by a majority of not less than three-fourths of the members of the company for the time being entitled to vote, present in person or by proxy at any general meeting of which notice specifying the intention to propose such resolution has been duly given, and such resolution has been confirmed by a majority of such members present in person or by proxy at a subsequent general meeting of which notice has been duly given, and held at an interval of not less than fourteen days nor more than one month from the date of the first meeting.

Q. In what manner are contracts on behalf of a company made ?

A. 1. Any contract which if made between private persons would be by law required to be in writing, and, if made according to English law, to be under seal, may be made on behalf of the company in writing under the common seal of the company, and such contract may be in the same manner varied or discharged.

2. Any contract which if made between private per-

sons would be by law required to be in writing, and signed by the parties charged therewith, may be made on behalf of the company in writing, signed by any person acting under the express or implied authority of the company, and such contract may in the same manner be varied or discharged.

3. Any contract which if made between private persons would by law be valid, although by parol and not in writing, may be made by parol on behalf of the company by any person acting under the express or implied authority of the company, and such contract may in the same way be varied or discharged.

Q. What provisions are made for the winding up of joint stock companies under the Joint Stock Companies Arrangement Act, 1870?

A. Provision is by previous statutes made for the winding up of joint stock companies, either by the court or voluntarily; and if *voluntarily*, the winding up may, by the order of the court, be subject to its supervision. And the Joint Stock Companies Arrangement Act, 1870 (33 & 34 Vict. c. 104), authorizes any compromise or arrangement to be made with the sanction of the court between a company in the course of being wound up and its creditors or any class of its creditors.

Q. Who are contributories under the Act, and how is their liability regulated?

A. All persons liable to contribute to the assets of a company under the Act, in the event of its being wound up, are called contributories. The liability of contributories is regulated by the rules set out in sect. 38 of the Act.

Q. What are the provisions of the Supreme Court of Judicature Act, 1875, as to the rules of bankruptcy being observed in the winding up of any company under the Companies Acts of 1862 and 1867?

A. The Act of 1875 provides that in the winding up of any company under the Companies Acts, 1862 and 1867, whose assets may prove insufficient for payment of its debts and liabilities and the costs of winding up, the same rules shall prevail and be observed as to the respective rights of secured and unsecured creditors, and as to debts and liabilities provable, and as to the valuation of annuities and future and contingent liabilities, as may be in force for the time being under the law of bankruptcy with respect to the estates of persons adjudged bankrupt.

Q. Are shares in joint stock companies *goods, wares* or *merchandise* within the 17th section of the Statute of Frauds?

A. They are not; so that they do not require a written memorandum for a contract for their sale when the value exceeds 10*l.*, and the buyer does not accept and receive any part, nor give something in earnest to bind the bargain or in part payment.

Q. State the principal provisions of the Friendly Societies Act, 1875.

A. This Act provides for the appointment of chief and assistant registrars of friendly societies, with a central office. Each friendly society is required to be registered; and no society assuring to any member a certain annuity shall be entitled to registry unless the tables of contributions for such assurance, properly certified by the actuary, be sent to the registrar with the application for registry. Every registered society must have a registered office and must appoint one or more trustees.

Q. In the case of a mortgage under this Act, what is the effect of a receipt under the hand of the trustees for the mortgage money?

A. Such a receipt, countersigned by the secretary, in the form contained in the third schedule to the Act, or specified by the rules of the society (such receipt being endorsed upon or annexed to such mortgage or other assurance), vacates the same and vests the property therein comprised in the person entitled to the equity of redemption of the same, without reconveyance or resurrender.

Q. What are the principal Acts now in force which regulate the formation and operation of industrial and provident societies?

A. They are all now consolidated into one Act, called the Industrial and Provident Societies Act, 1876 (39 & 40 Vict. c. 45).

Q. What is the effect of the Building Societies Act, 1874?

A. By this Act (37 & 38 Vict. c. 42, amended by 38 Vict. c. 9 and 40 & 41 Vict. c. 63) the laws relating to building societies have been consolidated and amended.

CHAPTER II.

OF PATENTS AND COPYRIGHTS.

Q. What is a patent, and by whom are letters patent granted, and for what term ?

A. A patent is the name usually given to a grant from the crown, by letters patent, of the exclusive privilege of making, using, exercising and vending some new invention. The granting of such letters patent is an ancient prerogative of the crown, a prerogative which remains unaffected by the Patent Law Amendment Act, 1852 (15 & 16 Vict. c. 83, s. 16); they may be granted for fourteen years or under.

Q. What are the principal alterations made by the Patent Law Amendment Act, 1852?

A. 1. The full term of fourteen years is usually granted; but it is now provided that all letters patent granted under the provisions of the above Act shall be made subject to the condition that the same shall be void at the expiration of three and seven years respectively from the date thereof, unless certain stamp duties be paid as mentioned in the Act.

2. The patent must be for " the working or making of new manufactures within this realm, which others, at the time of making such letters patent and grants, shall not use."

3. A patent must be granted " to the true and first inventor and inventors." If the original inventor should sell his secret to some other person, such person

cannot obtain letters patent for the invention in his own name; but the original inventor must obtain the letters patent and assign them to the other. Letters patent will be held to be void unless a complete specification be filed along with them, which must particularly describe and ascertain the nature of the invention and in what manner the same is to be performed. Letters patent must be registered in the manner prescribed in the Act.

Q. Can the patentee or assignee *disclaim* any part of the title of the invention or of the specification?

A. He may enter a disclaimer of any part either of the title of the invention or of the specification, stating the reason of such disclaimer, or enter a memorandum of any alteration in the title or specification, not being such disclaimer or such alteration as shall extend the exclusive right granted by the patent. Under these provisions letters patent originally void may in many cases be rendered valid, the disclaimer being read as part of the original title or specification.

Q. What is a license to use a patent?

A. In letters patent is usually a clause forbidding all persons from using the invention without the consent, license or agreement of the inventor, his executors, administrators or assigns, in writing, under hand and seal, first obtained. The granting of licenses to use a patent is one of the most profitable ways of turning it to account. All licenses are now required to be registered in the registry required to be kept by the Act of 1852.

Q. May letters patent be assigned? and what is the effect of such assignment?

A. They are freely assignable from one person to another, and the assignee by such assignment is placed in the same position as his assignor. Such assignments are now required to be registered under the Act of 1852.

Q. What is copyright, and what statute now regulates the law of copyright, and for how long does it continue?

A. Copyright is the exclusive right of multiplying copies of an original work or composition. The law of copyright is now regulated by the stat. 5 & 6 Vict. c. 45. By this Act the copyright of every book (which term includes, for the purposes of the Act, every pamphlet, sheet of letterpress, sheet of music, map, chart or plan) published after the passing of the Act, in the lifetime of the author, endures for his natural life, and for seven years from his death, or for forty-two years, whichever is the longer.

Q. How long does the copyright last in articles published in encyclopedias and reviews, &c.?

A. After the term of twenty-eight years from the first publication of any·such article the right of publishing the same in a separate form shall revert to the author for the remainder of the term given by the Act; and during such twenty-eight years the proprietor may not publish any such article separately without previously obtaining the consent of the author or his assigns.

Q. What copyright is there in prints, engravings, maps and charts?

A. For the term of twenty-eight years, to commence from the day of the first publishing thereof; which day, together with the proprietor's name, is to be truly engraved on each plate and printed on every print.

Q. What in original sculptures, models, copies and casts?

A. Fourteen years from their first putting forth or publishing the same, with a further term of fourteen years to the original maker if he shall be then living, provided that in every case the proprietor cause his name, with the date, to be put on every such sculpture, model, copy or cast before the same shall be put forth or published.

Q. What in paintings, drawings and lithographs?

A. For the term of the author's natural life (he being a British subject or resident within the dominions of the crown), and seven years after his death; and a register of proprietors of copyright in paintings, drawings and lithographs is established at Stationers' Hall, subject to similar regulations to that established for the registry of copyright in books.

Q. What are the statutes which regulate the law of international copyright? and what may the queen direct by Order in Council?

A. Stat. 7 & 8 Vict. c. 12, 25 & 26 Vict. c. 68, 15 & 16 Vict. c. 12, s. 6, and 38 Vict. c. 12. Her majesty is empowered, by Order in Council, to direct that the authors of dramatic pieces and musical compositions which shall, after a future time to be specified on such order, be first publicly performed in any foreign country to be named in such order, shall have the sole liberty of representing or performing in any part of the British dominions such dramatic pieces or musical compositions during such period as shall be defined in such order, not exceeding the period allowed in this country.

7*

Q. What copyright is granted for designs for articles of manufacture?

A. By statutes of the present reign a copyright has been granted to designs for articles of manufacture for the term of three years, one year or nine calendar months, according to the nature of the manufacture; and in pursuance of these Acts a registrar of designs for articles of manufacture has been appointed, by whom all designs to be protected by the Acts are required to be registered; and provision is also made for the transfer of the copyright in such designs by any writing purporting to be a transfer and signed by the proprietor, and also for the registration of transfers in a prescribed form.

Q. What are trade marks?

A. The marks often used by manufacturers to designate goods made by them resemble copyright as a subject of property, and the court will restrain a third person from passing off his own goods as those made by another, by the use of that other person's trade mark. By 25 & 26 Vict. c. 88, forging trade marks is made a misdemeanor, and there is now an implied warranty that all goods sold with a trade mark upon them are genuine. By the Trade Marks Registration Act, 1875 (38 & 39 Vict. c. 91, amended by 39 & 40 Vict. c. 33 and 40 and 41 Vict. c. 37), a register of trade marks is established. Trade marks must consist of one or more of the following essential particulars:—A name of an individual or firm printed, impressed or woven in some particular and distinctive manner; or a written signature or copy of a written signature of an individual or firm ; or a distinctive device, mark, heading, label or ticket ; and there may be added to any one or more of the said particulars any letters, words or figures or combination of any letters, words or figures.

Q. Define the term " goodwill."

A. The goodwill of a trade or business is often of very great value. It comprises every advantage which has been acquired by carrying on the business, whether connected with the premises in which the business has been carried on or with the name of the firm by whom it has been conducted.

PART IV.

OF PERSONAL ESTATE GENERALLY.

CHAPTER I.

OF SETTLEMENTS OF PERSONAL PROPERTY.

Q. What would be the effect of an assignment of any chattel, real or personal, to A. for his life, with remainder to another?

A. If any chattel, whether real or personal, were assigned to A. for his life, A. at once became entitled in law to the whole. But equity on his death would enforce the remainder over, which could be disposed of meanwhile; and if the property consisted of movable goods, equity would have compelled A. to furnish and sign an inventory of the goods and an undertaking to take proper care of them.

Q. What was the difference in case of a bequest by will of a term for life?

A. In a bequest by will of a term of years, the intention of the testator was carried into effect by the application of a doctrine similar to that of executory devises of real estates. The whole term of years was considered as vesting in the legatee for life, in the same manner as under an assignment by deed; but on his decease the term was held to shift away from him and to vest by way of executory bequest in the person to be next entitled.

Q. What are the principal objects of the Apportionment Act, 1870 ?

A. It provides that from and after the passing of that Act all rents, annuities, dividends and other periodical payments in the nature of income (whether reserved or made payable under an instrument in writing or otherwise) shall, like interest or money lent, be considered as accruing from day to day, and shall be apportionable in respect of time accordingly. Nothing in the Act contained is to render apportionable any annual sums made payable on policies of assurance of any description, or where it is expressly stipulated that no apportionment shall take place.

Q. Can an estate tail be created in personal property, and what would be the effect of a gift of personal property to A. and the heirs of his body ?

A. An estate tail cannot be created in personal property, neither does equity admit of any similar interest. Such gift will simply vest in A. the property given.

Q. Do the rules as to contingent remainders apply to contingent dispositions of personal property ?

A. No. As no estates can subsist in personal property it follows that the rules on which contingent remainders in freehold lands depend for their existence have never had any application to contingent dispositions of personal property ; as, if a gift of personal property be made to trustees in trust for A. for his life, and after his decease in trust for such son of A. as shall first attain the age of twenty-one years, it is immaterial whether such son attains that age in the lifetime of his father.

Q. Does the rule against perpetuities, which confirms executory interests within a life or lives in being and twenty-one years afterwards, apply to personal estate?

A. It applies equally to personal as to real estates.

Q. Does the restriction on accumulation imposed by the Thelluson Act apply to personalty?

A. The restriction on the accumulation of income applies to personal as well as to real estate.

Q. Do the same rules which apply to powers over real estate also apply to powers over personal property?

A. Yes; such as the formalities of the power must be complied with:

The relief afforded against defective executions.

Their execution by married women.

The execution of wills made under powers.

And their being included under a general devise.

Q. What was an *illusory* appointment, and are such appointments valid?

A. An *illusory* appointment was an appointment to any child of a very small share. The appointment of any share, however small, cannot now, as formerly, be set aside on the ground of its being illusory.

Q. Are exclusive appointments now void?

A. Formerly they were so if not authorized; this, however, has now been altered by a recent statute (37 & 38 Vict. c. 37), which enacts that no appointment thereinafter made under a power to appoint, amongst several objects, shall be invalid at law or in equity on the ground that any object of such power has been altogether excluded, unless the instrument creating the power declare the amount, from which no object of the power shall be excluded, or that some one or more object or objects of the power shall not be excluded.

Q. Does a power to appoint property to children authorize an appointment in favor of any grandchild of the appointor?

A. A power to appoint property to children does not authorize any interest in property to be appointed in favor of a grandchild. A power to appoint to children living at death of the father includes a child *in ventre sa mère*.

Q. What is meant by the hotchpot clause?

A. In default of or subject to any appointment that may be made, the property is usually divisible amongst the objects of the power, and a clause is inserted in order to prevent double portions, to the effect that any object to whom an appointment has been made must first bring such appointed share into hotchpot before sharing in the residue unappointed.

Q. When is an appointment in favor of the issue of a living child good?

A. This can only be done when the power authorizes an appointment to issue, or the child is of age, and is a party to and executes the deed by which the appointment is made.

Q. Can an appointment be made by a father to his child so that the former may derive a benefit from it?

A. No; that would be a fraud on the power, and would be void.

Q. Does the law as to perpetuity apply in the exercise of powers of appointment?

A. When the power of appointment is a general power, enabling the appointor to make a disposition in

favor of any object he may please, the property is evi-
dently not tied up so long as such a power exists over
it; and neither the reason nor the rule which forbids a
perpetuity has any application till some settlement is
made in exercise of such a power, but the rule applies
in the case of a special power from the date of its cre-
ation, and every limitation that *may* exceed the period
allowed is void.

Q. If a legacy be given to A., payable at twenty-one,
and A. dies under age, does that legacy lapse?

A. If a legacy be given to a person to be payable
when he attain the age of twenty-one, the legacy is considered to be immediately vested, and will accordingly
be payable to the administrator of the legatee in case he
should die under age.

Q. What new provisions were made by the statute 23
& 24 Vict. c. 145, s. 26, as to maintenance?

A. It provides that in all cases where it enables
trustees, holding property for an infant, either absolutely
or contingently on his attaining the age of twenty-one
years, or on the occurrence of any event previously to
his attaining that age, at their sole discretion to apply
for maintenance or education the whole or any part of
the income, or accumulation of income, to which such
infant *may be entitled* in respect of such property. This
enactment applies only to deeds executed and wills executed, or confirmed or revived by codicil executed, after
the passing of the Act, which took place on the 28th of
August, 1860.

Q. Is a married woman, having separate property,
liable for the maintenance of her children?

A. The Married Women's Property Act, 1870, now provides that a married woman, having separate property, shall be subject to all such liability for the maintenance of her children as a widow is now by law subject to for the maintenance of her children, provided that nothing in the Act shall relieve her husband from any liability at present imposed upon him by law to maintain her children.

Q. What description of securities are usually authorized in settlements of personal property?

A. In settlements of personal property it has long been usual to provide for the investment of the fund settled in the parliamentary stocks or public funds of Great Britain, or at interest upon government or real securities in England or Wales, but *not* in Ireland; and, at the present day, investments in railway debentures, preference shares, and other securities yielding a larger income are usually authorized.

Q. What authority has been given to trustees by the statute 22 & 23 Vict. c. 35, as regards investments?

A. Unless expressly forbidden, a power to invest in real securities in the United Kingdom, in bank stock of England or Ireland, or in East India stock.

Q. What powers are given under the Debenture Stock Act, 1871?

A. Trustees who have a power of investing in debenture bonds under the Act may invest in debenture stock.

Q. What is the peculiar effect of a direction to the trustee of a settlement to sell land?

A. This trust for sale converts the lands into money in the contemplation of equity; for it is a rule of equity that whatever is agreed to be done shall be considered as done already. In the words of Sir Thomas Sewell, "Nothing is better established than this principle, that money directed to be employed in the purchase of land, and land directed to be sold and turned into money, are to be considered that species of property into which they are directed to be converted."

Q. Can the parties interested elect to take the property as unconverted?

A. Yes, if they are of full age, and, if females, unmarried; and after such election, which may be inferred from acts as well as words, equity will consider the property as unconverted.

Q. Is a receipt clause now necessary in settlements?

A. By 22 & 23 Vict. c. 35, s. 23, it is enacted that the *bonâ fide* payment to and receipt of any person to whom any *purchase or mortgage* money is payable, upon any express or implied trust, effectually discharges the person paying the same from seeing to the application thereof; and the same is declared by 23 & 24 Vict. c. 145, with respect to a receipt in writing for any moneys payable to trustees under their trust.

Q. What is the effect of the statute of 23 & 24 Vict. c. 145 as regards the power to appoint new trustees?

A. This Act confers a power to appoint new trustees upon the person appointed by the instrument for such purpose (if ready and willing to act); if not, upon the surviving or acting trustees or trustee, or the acting executors or administrators of the last surviving or last retiring trustee, in the event of any trustee dying, going to reside beyond the seas, desiring to be discharged, refusing or becoming incapable to act in the execution of the trusts.

Q. State the principal provisions of the Trustees Act, 1850, and the statute 15 & 16 Vict. c. 55.

A. The Trustees Act, 1850, empowers the Court of Chancery to appoint a new trustee in all cases where it is inexpedient, difficult or impracticable to do so without the assistance of that court, and either in substitution for or in addition to any existing trustee, and whether there be any existing trustee or not. Provision is also made for the appointment of a new trustee in lieu of any trustee who may have been convicted of felony, and for the infancy, lunacy or idiotcy of any trustee or executor, and for his being out of the jurisdiction of the court or not being found, and for its being uncertain whether he is living or dead, and for his neglecting or refusing to transfer any stock or to receive the dividends or income thereof, or to sue for or recover any chose in action. In the event of bankruptcy of any trustee the Court of Chancery is empowered to appoint a new trustee in his place.

Q. Can a trustee who is a solicitor charge for his work done by him in the business of the trust?

A. He cannot receive payment for his professional trouble incurred in the business of the trust unless he expressly stipulate before accepting the office that he shall be permitted to do so, or unless his charges be paid by the *cestui que trust* with full knowledge that they might have been resisted.

Q. What is the effect of the statute 22 & 23 Vict. c. 35 as to the insertion of certain clauses in ordinary settlements?

A. In all ordinary settlements clauses used to be inserted for the indemnity and reimbursement of trustees, to the effect that they should not be answerable the one for the other of them, or for signing receipts for the sake of conformity or for involuntary loss; and that they might reimburse themselves out of the trust funds all costs and expenses in relation to the trust. The above Act enacts that every deed, will or other instrument creating a trust, either expressly or by implication, shall be deemed to contain these clauses.

Q. What are the provisions of the statute 10 & 11 Vict. c. 96 as to the power of trustees with regard to trust funds in their hands, and what jurisdiction have the county courts?

A. By this Act all trustees, executors, administrators or other persons having in their hands any moneys belonging to any trust whatsoever (or the major part of them) may pay the same, with the privity of the paymaster-general, into court. By 30 & 31 Vict. c. 142, where the fund does not exceed in amount or value the sum of five hundred pounds, jurisdiction is now given to the county courts.

Q. Is marriage a good consideration? and what constitutes a voluntary settlement, and is it void as against creditors?

A. Marriage is a valuable consideration. Every settlement, therefore, made by parties of full age previously to and in consideration of marriage, or made subsequently in pursuance of written articles executed before, stands on the footing of a purchase, and has equal validity. A voluntary settlement is one not made for

valuable consideration, and is liable to be defeated by
the creditors of the settlor if he was so much indebted
at the time as to bring the settlement within the provision of the statute of 13 Eliz. c. 5.

Q. Is a voluntary settlement binding upon the settlor
when there is no power of revocation? and what difference does it make when such settlement is made for the
settlor's own benefit?

A. Although a voluntary settlement may be defeated
by creditors, yet when once completed it is binding
on the settlor, who cannot by any means undo it. If
the object of the settlor is merely his own benefit or
convenience, the settlement will be revocable by him at
his pleasure.

Q. What stamp duty is chargeable on a settlement of
stock or of a policy of assurance?

A. Five shillings per cent. on the value of the stock
or on the sum secured by the policy, if there is a provision for keeping up the policy, otherwise on the value
of the policy at the time of settlement.

CHAPTER II.

OF JOINT OWNERSHIP AND JOINT LIABILITY.

Q. Are the four unities of *possession*, *interest*, *title*
and *time*, which characterize a joint tenancy of real
estate, also applicable to a joint ownership of chattels?

A. There may be a joint ownership of any kind of

personal property in the same manner as there may be a joint tenancy of real estate; and the four unities of *possession, interest, title* and *time* also apply.

Q. What is the effect of a release by one of several obligees in the case of a joint bond or covenant?

A. If a bond or covenant be given or made to two or more jointly, they must all join in suing upon it, and a release by one of them to the obligor is sufficient to bar them all.

Q. In what case does an exception occur in the right of survivorship between joint owners, and what is the rule with regard to land purchased by them?

A. In the case of partners in trade, the share of the deceased in all chattels in possession vests in the executor or administrator. With respect to land purchased for partnership purposes, equity holds the survivor a trustee of the share of the deceased for his executor or administrator.

Q. Is joint ownership favored in equity, and what is the result in case of a mortgage where the money is advanced by two persons and one of them dies?

A. Joint ownership is not favored in equity on account of the right of survivorship which attaches to it. If, therefore, two persons advance money by way of mortgage or otherwise, and take the security to themselves jointly and one of them die, the survivor will be a trustee in equity for the representatives of the deceased, of the share advanced by him.

Q. In the case of wills, what is the rule as to words which will be sufficient to give to each of several legatees a tenancy in common?

A. The rule is that any words which denote an intention to give to each of the legatees a distinct interest in the subject of gift will be sufficient to make them tenants in common ; as "equally to be divided between them," or simply "between them," or "in joint and equal proportions," or "equally," or "respectively," or "to be enjoyed alike."

Q. What unity have owners in common of personal estate ?

A. Owners in common of personal estate, like tenants in common of lands, have merely a unity of possession. The interest of one may be larger or smaller than that of the other, one having, for instance, one-third, and the other two-thirds, of the property. So the title need not be the same, as one may have been originally a joint tenant with a third person, who may have severed the joint tenancy by assigning his moiety to the other.

Q. What is the best form of a joint and several covenant ?

A. "And the said A. B., C. D., E. F. and G. H. do hereby for themselves, their heirs, executors and administrators jointly, and any two or three of them do hereby for themselves, their heirs, executors and administrators jointly, and each of them doth hereby for himself respectively, and for his respective heirs, executors and administrators, cóvenant," &c. In all cases of joint and several liability each party is individually liable, and may be sued alone for the whole debt ; or, if the creditor please, he may sue them all jointly. In consequence of the joint liability, a release of one of the debtors will discharge them all.

Q. State some of the principal incidents of a partnership.

A. At law the liability of partners is joint only as to debts incurred by the partnership, so that they ought all to be joined as defendants to an action at law for recovering any such debt. But a dormant partner, whose name may or may not be known, may either be joined or not at the pleasure of the creditor, unless the contract be under seal; in which case, as the deed is itself the contract, and not merely evidence of it, those only can be sued on it who have sealed and delivered it. In equity, in favor of creditors, all partnership debts are considered to be both joint and several.

Q. What is the rule as to payment of debts on bankruptcy of a firm?

A. The joint assets of the firm are, in the first place, liable to the partnership debts; and the separate estate of each partner is, in the first place, liable to his separate debts, which must be paid in full out of such separate estate before any of it can be applied towards payment of the debts of the partnership.

Q. In what cases can a person now receive part of the profits of a business without being responsible for the debts?

A. By the Partnership Act, 28 & 29 Vict. c. 86, in the following cases:—

1. A person may advance money to a person engaged in any undertaking, and receive interest, varying with the profits or a share of profits.

2. A servant or agent may receive a share of such profits.

3. A widow or child of a deceased partner of a trader may receive, by way of annuity, a portion of such profits.

4. And a vendor of the business may receive, by way of annuity or otherwise, a portion of such profits, as a consideration for the goodwill thereof.

Q. What are the liabilities of partners in relation to each other in the ordinary course of business?

A. Each incurs liability from the acts and dealings of the other in the ordinary course of business.

CHAPTER III.

OF A WILL.

Q. Can an infant now make a will?

A. No will made by a person under twenty-one is now valid.

Q. What is the statute which now regulates the making and operation of wills, and what exception is made in favor of soldiers and seamen?

A. The Wills Act of 1837 (1 Vict. c. 26) requires it to be in writing, signed at the foot or end thereof by the testator, or by some other person in his presence or by his direction, and such signature must be made or acknowledged by the testator in the presence of two or more witnesses present at the same time, who must attest the will in the presence of the testator. Exception is made in favor of soldiers being in actual military service, that is, on expeditions, and of mariners and seamen, being at sea, who may dispose of their personal estate as they might have done before the making of the Act. The wills of soldiers may accordingly be made by an unattested writing, or by mere nuncupative testament or declaration of their will by word of mouth, made before a sufficient number of witnesses. But the wills of petty officers and seamen require attestation and witnessing by Act of Parliament, so far as relates to any wages, pay, prize money or other moneys payable by the Admiralty, and the wills of such persons are also guarded by other requisitions in order to prevent their being imposed upon.

Q. How may a will be revoked?

A. A will may be revoked by marriage of the testator or testatrix (which will of itself form a revocation), or by another will or codicil executed in the manner thereby required, or by some writing declaring an intention to revoke the same, and executed in the manner in which a will is thereby required to be executed, or by burning, tearing or otherwise destroying the same, by the testator, or by some person in his presence and by his direction, with the intention of revoking the same.

Q. What is now enacted by 24 & 25 Vict. c. 114, with respect to wills of personal estate made by a British subject out of the United Kingdom?

A. That such wills (whatever may be the domicil of the testator) shall be held to be well executed if made according to the forms required either (1), by the law of the place where made; or (2), the law of the place where the person was domiciled when the will was made;

or (3), the law then in force in that part of her majesty's dominions where he had his domicil of origin.

Q. What is the nature of a *donatio mortis causâ*?

A. It is a gift made in contemplation of death, to be absolute only in case of the death of the giver. Being a gift, it can be made only of chattels, the property in which passes by delivery. It is revocable by the donor during his life, and after his decease it is subject to his debts, and it is also liable to legacy duty.

Q. Is the appointment of an executor to a will of personalty now essential?

A. Formerly it was essential, and now it is usual and proper to do so; whereas, under a devise of landed property, the lands pass to the devisee, and the intervention of an executor is quite unnecessary and inapplicable, all the personal property vests in the executor on the death, and not even a specific legacy will vest in the legatee until the executor has assented to the bequest.

Q. Can an infant be appointed executor?

A. If an infant be appointed an executor he will not be allowed to exercise his office during his minority; but during this time the administration of the goods of the deceased will be granted to the guardian of the infant or to such person as the Court of Probate may think fit. Such person is called an administrator *durante minore ætate*.

Q. Can a married woman be appointed an executrix, and if she is, what is the effect?

A. A married woman cannot accept the office of executrix without her husband's consent, and, having accepted it with his consent, she is unable, without his

concurrence, to perform any act of administration which
may be to his prejudice; whilst he, on the other hand,
may release debts due to the deceased, or make assignment of the deceased's personal estate without his wife's
concurrence.

Q. What is an *executor de son tort?*

A. If any person not duly authorized should intermeddle with the goods of the testator, or do any other
act relating to the office of executor, he thereby becomes
an executor of his own wrong, or, as it is called in law
French, an executor *de son tort.* He is liable for the
assets which come to his hands, but he can derive no
benefit from his office; he cannot retain his own debt in
preference to others.

Q. Supposing a regularly-appointed executor to be a
creditor of testator, has he a right to retain his own debt
in preferment to other debts of the same degree?

A. Yes; he may do so.

Q. Must a will of personalty be proved, and where?

A. All wills of personalty must be proved in the Probate, Divorce and Admiralty Division of the High Court.
In this division of the court the will itself is deposited,
and a copy of the will which is given by the court to
the executor on proving, denominated the probate copy,
is the only proper evidence of the right of the executor
to intermeddle with the personal estate of his testator.
Before probate, however, the executor may perform all
ordinary acts of administration, such as receiving and
giving receipts for debts due to the testator, paying the
debts owing by the testator, and selling and assigning
any part of the personal estate. But when evidence is

required of his right to intermeddle, the probate is the only valid proof; without it, therefore, no action or suit can be maintained, although proceedings may be commenced before and carried up to the point where the evidence is required. Any will may now be proved in the principal registry, without regard to the abode of the testator. But if the testator had at the time of his death a fixed place of abode within any district, his will may be proved in the registry of that district.

Q. How is a will proved?

A. When the attestation is in proper form and the validity of the will is not disputed, it is *proved* by the simple oath of the executor that he believes the will to be the true last will and testament of the deceased. When the required formalities have not been complied with, an affidavit, in addition to the executor's oath, is required from one of the subscribing witnesses, that the will was executed in compliance with the statute. Probate in either of the above modes is termed probate in *common form*. But if the validity of the will should be disputed or any dispute should be anticipated by the executor, the will is proved *in solemn form per testes.* In this case both the witnesses are sworn and examined, and such other evidence taken as the circumstances require, in the presence of the widow and next of kin of the testator, and all others pretending to have any interest, who are cited to be present, to see the proceedings. When a will has once been proved in this form it is finally established.

Q. In respect of what property is probate duty payable?

A. In respect of the whole of the personal and movable estate and effects of the deceased in the United Kingdom. The probate duty is in the first place paid on the whole value of the personal estate of the testator without allowing for his debts; and after the debts are paid, a return of part of the probate duty is made according to the value to which the estate may be reduced by the payment of the debts. But where leasehold estates are the sole security by way of mortgage for any debts due from the deceased, the amount of such mortgage debts may be deducted from the value of the said leasehold estate.

Q. After the probate, what are the powers of executors as to payment of debts, &c. ?

A. After the will has been proved, it is the duty of the executor to pay the testator's debts out of the personal estate, to which such executor becomes entitled by virtue of his office.

Q. When is interest payable on a legacy?

A. All such general legacies which remain unpaid after a year from testator's death carry interest at the rate of 4l. per cent. per annum. But if the legacy be given by a parent, or by a person *in loco parentis*, to a legatee under the age of twenty-one years, interest is given from the death of the testator for the maintenance of the legatee, in the absence of any other provision for that purpose.

Q. What rates of duty are payable on legacies?

A. The amount of legacy duty varies according to the degree of relationship which the legatee bore to the deceased. Where the legacy is to a child or lineal descendant, or to the father or mother of any lineal ancestor of the deceased, the duty is 1*l.* per cent. If to a brother, sister or their descendants, 3*l.* per cent. If to a brother or sister of the father or mother or their descendants, 5*l.* per cent. If to a brother or sister of a grandfather or grandmother or their descendants, 6*l.* per cent. And if to any other person or to any stranger in blood, the duty is 10*l.* per cent. But where any person chargeable with legacy duty shall have been married to any wife or husband of nearer consanguinity than himself or herself to the deceased, the smaller rate of duty only is payable. And the husband or wife of the deceased is exempt from all legacy duty, and so, also, are the royal family.

Q. State the difference between specific, demonstrative and general legacies.

A. A specific legacy is a bequest of a specific part of the testator's personal estate; it has priority in case of deficiency of assets, but it is liable to ademption.

A demonstrative legacy is a gift by will of a certain sum directed to be paid out of a specific fund; it is not liable to ademption.

A general legacy is one payable only out of the general assets of the testator, and is liable to abatement in case of a deficiency of such assets to pay the testator's debts and other legacies.

Q. When is a legacy to a creditor a satisfaction of the *debt,* and when of a *portion ?*

A. If the legacy be equal to or greater than the amount of the debt. But if it be less than the debt, or payable at a different time, or of a different nature from the debt, or if the debt be contracted subsequently to the date of the will, or if the will contain an express direction for payment of debts and legacies, the legacy will not be a satisfaction. When a sum of money is due to a child by way of portion the inclination of the courts is against double portions; and a legacy to such a child is accordingly regarded as a satisfaction of the portion, either in part or in whole, notwithstanding such legacy may be less than the portion, or payable at a different period.

Q. What are the chief objects of the Statute of Mortmain?

A. By a statute of George the Second, commonly called the Mortmain Act, no hereditaments nor any money stock in the public funds, or other personal estate whatsoever, to be laid out in the purchase of hereditaments, can be conveyed or settled for any charitable uses (with a few exceptions) otherwise than by deed, with certain formalities mentioned in the Act. And all gifts of hereditaments, or of any estate or interest therein, or of any charge or incumbrance affecting or to affect any hereditaments, or of any personal estate to be laid out in the purchase of any hereditaments, or of any estate or interest therein, or of any charge or incumbrance affecting or to affect the same, to or in trust for any charitable uses whatsoever, are rendered void if made in any form than by the Act is directed.

Q. When can illegitimate children take under a will?

A. A child *primâ facie* means a legitimate child; accordingly an illegitimate child can never take under a gift to children unless it be clear upon the terms of the will, or according to the state of facts at the making of it, that legitimate children never could have taken it. An illegitimate child may, however, take under any gift in which he is sufficiently identified as the object of the testator's bounty. Thus a bequest to the child of which a woman is now pregnant is good; and if illegitimate children have acquired the reputation of being the children of the testator or any other person, and it appear by necessary implication on the face of the will that such persons were intended in a bequest to children, they will be entitled, not on account of their being children, but on account of their reputation as such.

Q. From what time does a will take effect?

A. A will of personal estate has always been considered as speaking from the death of the testator, and it is now expressly enacted that it shall do so unless a contrary intention appear in the will, when all lapsed legacies fall into the residuary bequest, if any.

Q. In what cases will a legacy lapse, and if it lapses, what becomes of it? And what distinction is made as regards legacies to children?

A. A legacy will lapse by the death of the legatee in the testator's lifetime, although given to the legatee, his executors, administrators and assigns. If any legacy lapse it will fall into the residue and belong to the residuary legatee. In the case of children who die leaving issue living at testator's death the legacy would not lapse, but shall take effect as if the death of such person had happened immediately after the death of the testator, unless a contrary intention shall appear by the will.

8*

Q. Supposing there is no residuary legatee, what becomes of the residue?

A. Formerly, after payment of the testator's debts and legacies, the residue of the personal estate belonged to the executor for his own benefit; but now, by 11 Geo. 4 and 1 Will. 4, c. 40, it is enacted that when any person shall die having by will or codicil appointed an executor, such executor shall be deemed by the courts of equity to be a trustee for the person or persons (if any) who would be entitled to the estate under the Statute of Distributions, in respect of any residue not expressly disposed of, unless it shall appear by the will or any codicil thereto that the person so appointed executor was intended to take such residue beneficially.

CHAPTER IV.

OF INTESTACY.

Q. To whom was the grant of administration usually made?

A. By 21 Hen. 8, c. 5, administration might be granted to the widow of the deceased or to the next of his kin, or to both, as the ordinary thought good; but the widow was usually preferred, and a joint grant was so seldom made that the powers of co-administrators appear still a matter of doubt. In granting administration to the next of kin the courts were guided by the right to the property to be administered. In default of the next of kin a creditor might, by custom, administer, on the ground that he could not be paid his debt until representation were made to the deceased.

Q. What are the statutes which now regulate the administration of the effects of intestates?

A. The Court of Probate Act, 1857 (20 & 21 Vict. c. 77, amended by 21 & 22 Vict. c. 95), abolished the whole of the jurisdiction which the ecclesiastical courts formerly had over the effects of intestates; and administration of the effects of deceased persons, formerly granted by those courts, is now granted by the Probate, Divorce and Admiralty Division of the High Court of Justice, in the same manner as the probate of wills; and on death of a person intestate, his personal estate vests in the president of the said division of the High Court.

Q. What court now has jurisdiction in the case where intestate's whole estate and effects do not exceed in value 100l.?

A. By recent statutes (36 & 37 Vict. c. 52 and 38 & 39 Vict. c. 27) facilities have been given to the widows and children of deceased intestates, and to the children of intestate widows whose whole estate and effects shall not exceed in value 100l., for taking out letters of administration to their effects, by application to the registrar of the county court within the district of which the intestate had his or her fixed place of abode at the time of death.

Q. What are the rights and powers of an administrator?

A. An administrator, when appointed, has the same right and power over the personal estate of the intestate as his executors would have had if he had made a will, and this right and power relate back to the time of intestate's decease. He has also the privilege of retaining his debt in preference to others of the same degree.

Q. Within what time should distribution be made by an administrator of the assets of an intestate?

A. The same period, viz., a year, as is allowed to an executor.

Q. What is administration *cum testamento annexo*?

A. Where a will has been made, but the executors have renounced, or died before the testator, the court will appoint the person having the greatest interest in the effects, generally the residuary legatee, to administer the same according to the directions of the will. This is called administration *cum testamento annexo*.

Q. What is administration " *de bonis non* "?

A. The office of administrator is not transmissible like the office of executor. On the decease of an administrator before he has distributed all the effects of the intestate a new administrator must be appointed; for the executor or administrator of such administrator has no right to intermeddle. So, if an executor should die intestate, without having completely distributed the testator's effects, an administrator must be appointed to distribute, according to the will of the testator, such of his effects as were not distributed by the deceased executor. In each of the above cases the administration is called " *de bonis non*."

Q. After payment of an intestate's debts, how is the application or distribution of his effects now regulated?

A. By the Statutes of Distribution (22 & 23 Car. 2, c. 10; 1 Jac. 2, c. 17, s. 7), by which statutes the rights of the relations of the deceased appear to have been first definitely ascertained and rendered legally available.

Q. What share does the widow take when there are children, and what when none?

A. In the first case the widow takes one-third and the children two-thirds; in the latter the widow takes half and the next of kin the other half, children as between themselves having to bring any advances into hotchpot.

Q. How far are children of next of kin entitled to take their deceased parent's share?

A. Beyond brothers' and sisters' children no right of representation belongs to the children of relatives.

Q. How are degrees of kindred traced in the distribution of an intestate's personal estate?

A. No preference is given to males over females, nor to the paternal over the maternal line, nor to the whole over the half blood, as in the case of the descent of real estate, nor do the issue stand in the place of the ancestor. The degrees of kindred are reckoned according to the civil law, both upwards to the ancestor and downwards to the issue, each generation counting for a degree. Thus, from father to son, or son to father, is one degree; from grandfather to grandson, or from grandson to grandfather, is two degrees; and from brother to brother is also two degrees—namely, one upwards to the father, and one downwards to the other son.

Q. Are there any customs still peculiar to the city of London and province of York as to the mode of distribution?

A. No; the statute 19 & 20 Vict. c. 94 altogether abolished *all customary* modes of administration *which formerly* existed in the above places.

CHAPTER V.

THE MUTUAL RIGHTS OF HUSBAND AND WIFE.

Q. Is there any, and what, difference between the laws of real and personal property as regards attempted restraint on marriage?

A. Real estate is governed by the rules of the common law; but personal estate, when bequeathed by will, has long been subject to the jurisdiction of the ecclesiastical courts. Some restrictions on marriage, which are valid when applied to a gift of real estate, are void when attempted to be imposed on a gift of personal property. The rules respecting real and personal estate so far agree that a condition annexed to the gift of either, that a person shall not marry at all, is void; but a gift of either, during manhood, is good.

Q. What is the effect of a gift, with a condition that it shall be forfeited if the donee marry without the consent of certain persons?

A. If the gift be of real estate, or of money charged on real estate, it will cease in the event of marriage without the required consent. But if it be a bequest of personal property, the condition is regarded as merely *in terrorem*, and void, unless accompanied by a bequest over to some other person, on the marriage taking place without consent.

Q. What provisions as to settlements by infants upon marriage have been made by 18 & 19 Vict. c. 43? and what is required to make such settlement binding?

A. This Act empowers every infant not under twenty if a male, and not under seventeen if a female, to settle his or her property, whether real or personal, upon marriage, provided the sanction of the Court of Chancery be obtained.

Q. What beneficial alterations in the law respecting the property of married women have been made by the Married Women's Property Act, 1870?

A. Formerly all the personal property of the wife became absolutely the husband's on his reducing it into possession, but this Act (33 & 34 Vict. c. 93) provides (*vide* s. 7) that where any woman married after the passing of the Act shall, during her marriage, become entitled to any personal property as next of kin, or one of the next of kin of an intestate, such property shall belong to the woman for her separate use (subject to any settlement affecting the same).

Q. What are paraphernalia, and in what respect do they differ from the wife's other personal chattels?

A. The wife's paraphernalia consist of her apparel and ornaments suitable to her rank and degree; and gifts made by the husband to his wife of jewels or trinkets, to be worn by her as ornaments, are considered as part of her paraphernalia. These articles, equally with the wife's other personal chattels, may be disposed of by the husband in his lifetime, and (with the exception of the wife's necessary clothing) are also liable to his debts. But paraphernalia differ from the wife's other personal chattels in this respect, that the husband, though he may dispose of them in his lifetime, has no power to bequeath them away from his wife by his will.

Q. What are the rights of the husband as regards his wife's choses in action?

A. With regard to choses in action, whether legal or equitable, the same rule applies as to the rights of the husband, viz., that if he can get them into his possession during the coverture he has a right to keep them, otherwise they will belong to his wife.

Q. What exceptions to the rule were made by the Married Women's Property Act, 1870?

A. The wages and earnings of any married woman, acquired or gained by her after the passing of the Act, in any employment, occupation or trade in which she is engaged, or carries on separately from her husband; also any money or property so acquired by her through the exercise of any literary, scientific or artistic skill, and all investment of such earnings, &c.; also any deposit in a savings bank, or any annuity granted by the Commissioners for the Reduction of the National Debt, in the name of a married woman or of a woman who may marry after such deposit or grant, shall be deemed to be her separate property, and shall be accounted for and paid to her as if she were an unmarried woman. The Act also contains several other provisions as to money in the funds, shares, or stock in companies, in friendly, or building, or loan societies, &c.

Q. In what cases may a married woman maintain an action in her own name?

A. For the recovery of any wages, earnings, money and property by the Act declared to be her separate property, or of any property belonging to her before marriage, and which the husband shall by writing under his hand have agreed with her shall belong to her after marriage as her separate property; and she shall have in her own name the same remedies, both civil and criminal, against all persons whomsoever for the protection and security thereof as if the same belonged to her as an unmarried woman.

Q. What are the rights of the husband as regards the legal choses in action belonging to his wife?

A. Of all these the husband has a right to receive payment, and should payment be refused him he may sue for them in the joint name of himself and his wife; but bills and notes of the wife payable to order, being transferable by endorsement, may be transferred by the husband alone, or sued for in his own name. All such legal choses in action as accrued to the wife after her marriage may be sued for by the husband, either in the joint names of himself and his wife, or in his own name only; but if the wife has really no interest, he cannot, of course, make use of her name.

Q. What is the rule as to the wife's equitable choses in action, and what is the wife's equity to a settlement?

A. All kinds of property, including both freehold estates and chattels real, vested in trustees, who were formerly answerable only to the Court of Chancery, are subject to a rule of equity, by which equitable choses in action are mainly distinguishable from such as are merely legal. This rule is, that the court will not assist, nor, if the wife should dissent, will it allow, the husband to recover or receive any property of his wife recoverable only in the Chancery Division of the High Court, without his settling a due proportion of such property on his wife and children. This is termed the wife's equity for a settlement. In fixing the proportion to be settled, a prior settlement will always be taken into account. Where there is no previous settlement, the proportion usually required to be settled on the wife is one-half, and sometimes the court has gone so far as to require a settlement of the whole fund.

Q. What is the effect of stat. 20 & 21 Vict. c. 57 as to the disposition of a married woman's reversionary interests?

A. Every married woman, with the concurrence of her husband, may by deed dispose of every future or reversionary interest, whether vested or contingent, of such married woman, or her husband in her right, in any personal estate to which she shall be entitled under any instrument (except her marriage settlement) *made after the 31st December*, 1857 (unless given to her separate use without power of anticipation); also to release or extinguish any power in regard to any such personal estate; also to release her equity to a settlement. But every such disposition must be separately acknowledged by her in the same manner as required by the Fines and Recoveries Act, 3 & 4 Will. 4, c. 74.

Q. What are the principal provisions of the stat. 37 & 38 Vict. c. 50, cited as the Married Women's Property Act (1870) Amendment Act, 1874?

A. It repeals so much of the Married Women's Property Act, 1870, as enacts that a husband shall not be liable for the debts of his wife contracted before marriage, so far as respects marriages which shall take place after the passing of the Act; and provides that a husband and wife married after that time may be jointly sued for such debt. When a husband and wife are sued jointly, if it appears that the husband is liable for the debt or damages recovered, or any part thereof, the judgment to the extent of the amount for which the husband is liable shall be a joint judgment against the husband and wife, and as to the residue, if any, of such debt or damages, the judgment shall be a separate judgment against the wife.

Q. To what extent is the husband liable under the last-mentioned statute as to the assets of his wife?

A. 1. The value of the personal estate in possession of the wife, which shall have vested in the husband.

2. The value of the choses in action of the wife which the husband shall have reduced into possession, or which with reasonable diligence he might have reduced into possession.

3. The value of the chattels real of the wife, which shall have vested in the husband and wife.

4. The value of the rents and profits of the real estate of the wife, which the husband received or with reasonable diligence might have received.

5. The value of the husband's estate or interest in any property, real or personal, which the wife, in contemplation of the marriage with him, shall have transferred to him or to any other person.

6. The value of any property, real or personal, which the wife, in contemplation of her marriage with the husband, shall, with his consent, have transferred to any person with the view of defeating or delaying her existing creditors.

Q. When may a married woman dispose of her personal estate by will?

A. By the husband giving her authority to dispose of such estate or any part of it by her will; and such will will be binding and valid on the husband if he once allow it to be proved. But during the wife's lifetime, and even after her death until probate of the will, this authority may be revoked; and if the husband should die before the wife, such a will would not be binding on the wife's next of kin.

Q. What is the effect of trusts for the wife's separate use?

A. When personal estate is so given, the wife has the same powers of ownership as if she were a *feme sole;* she may accordingly dispose of such property without her husband's concurrence, either in her lifetime or by her will. But should she die in his lifetime without having made any disposition, her husband will become entitled to it either in his marital right or as her administrator, according as the property may be in possession or in action. A trust for a woman's *separate use* is properly and technically created by means of the words "separate use." But a direction that her receipt alone shall be a sufficient discharge is sufficient. A gift, however, to a woman for her sole use has now been decided not to create a trust for her separate use, unless aided by the context.

Q. What is the effect of a clause against anticipation?

A. When property is settled to the separate use of a married woman, this deprives the woman of the power of disposition over it during coverture.

Q. In the event of a separation between husband and wife, who is entitled to the custody of infant children, and what alteration in the law has been recently made in that respect?

A. The custody of infant children in such case belongs by law to the father as the natural guardian. It is now provided by stat. 36 Vict. c. 12 (24th April, 1873) that after the passing of that Act it shall be lawful for the Court of Chancery, upon hearing the petition by her next friend of the mother of any infant or infants under sixteen years of age, to order that the petitioner shall have access to such infant or infants, and to order that such infant or infants be delivered to the mother and remain in or under her custody or control, or that they remain therein until such infant shall attain such age, not exceeding sixteen, as the court shall direct; and further, to order that such custody or control shall be subject to such regulation as regards access by the father or guardian of such infant or infants, and otherwise as the court shall deem proper.

Q. What protection is now given to a wife deserted by her husband?

A. She may apply to a magistrate or to the court, or a judge ordinary thereof, for an order to protect any money or property she may acquire by her own lawful industry, and property which she may become possessed of after such desertion, against her husband or his creditors. And, in such case, such earnings and property will belong to herself, as if she were a *feme sole*.

Q. In case of a judicial separation, is the wife considered as a *feme sole* with respect to her property?

A. From the date of the sentence, and whilst separated, the wife is to be considered as a *feme sole* with
respect to her property, whether held beneficially or as
executrix, administratrix or trustee; and also for the
purposes of contract; and wrongs, and injuries, and
suing, and being sued in any legal proceeding; and her
property may be disposed of by her in all respects as a
feme sole; and, on her decease, the same will, in case
she shall die intestate, go as it would have gone if her
husband had then been dead.

PART V.

OF TITLE.

Q. In the case of money and negotiable securities is it necessary for a payer to show any title?

A. No title at all is required to be shown by the payer on any *bonâ fide* transaction; but if *mala fides* can be shown on the part of the party receiving it, or such gross negligence as amounts to evidence thereof, the true owner may recover the property, provided its identity can be ascertained.

Q. What is a market overt?

A. With regard to ordinary choses in possession, a valid title to them is usually obtained by a purchase in open market, or *market overt*, although no property therein may have been possessed by the vendor. And every shop in the city of London is market overt for goods usually sold therein; but if goods are stolen, and the thief is prosecuted to conviction, the property in the goods reverts to the original owner, notwithstanding an intermediate sale in market overt. (See 24 & 25 Vict. c. 96, s. 100.)

Q. What is the effect of a power of attorney?

A. When one man is appointed the agent of another for any particular purpose by power of attorney, his authority must be strictly pursued, otherwise his principal will not be bound. By modern Acts of Parliament a more extended authority has, for the convenience of commerce, been conferred on factors and agents. The general effect of these Acts is to render valid sales and pledges made by factors or agents, notwithstanding any notice of the fact of their being merely factors or agents, provided the party dealing with them have no notice that they are acting without authority or *malâ fide*.

Q. What warranty arises on the sale of goods?

A. None, unless expressly given or implied by the custom of trade or the nature of the contract; as in a contract to furnish goods for a particular purpose, a warranty is implied that they are fit for that purpose. A warranty given subsequent to the sale is void for want of consideration.

Q. What are the principal provisions of the Statute of Limitations (21 Jac. 1, c. 16)?

A. By this statute all actions of trespass, detinue and replevin for goods or cattle must be brought within six years next after the cause of such action. But if the person entitled to any such action be under age, *feme covert*, or *non compos mentis*, such person shall be at liberty to bring the same action within *six* years after the disability is removed. The disabilities of absence beyond seas and imprisonment have been abolished by a recent statute.

Q. Within what time are mortgage moneys, judgments and legacies now recoverable?

A. No action or suit can be brought to recover the same but within *twenty years* next after a present right to receive the same shall have accrued to some person capable of giving a discharge for or release of the same, unless in the meantime some part of the principal money or some interest thereon shall have been paid, or some acknowledgment of the right thereto shall have been given in writing, signed by the person by whom the same shall be payable, or his agent, to the person entitled thereto, or his agent; and in such case such action or suit must be brought within twenty years thereafter.

Q. How has this period been altered by the Real Property Limitation Act, 1874?

A. This Act, which comes into force on the first day of January, 1879, reduced the above period of twenty years to twelve years, except in the case of the personal estate, or any share of an intestate's personal estate.

Q. Within what time must arrears of rent or interest charged on real estate, or in respect of any legacy, be recovered?

A. Within six years after becoming due, or of an acknowledgment in writing given to the person entitled thereto, or his agent, signed by the party to be charged, or his agent; but if secured by deed, an action may be brought within twenty years.

Q. Does the statute continue to run on death of the debtor?

A. Yes, and it does not stop until administration be taken out.

Q. Is any executor or administrator bound to plead the Statute of Limitations to any debt or demand?

A. He is not; but may if he please pay the same, notwithstanding the time limited by the statute may have expired. But if the estate be administered in the Chancery Division of the High Court, any party to the suit is competent to take the objection, although the executor may not have insisted on it.

Q. Will any longer period be allowed where the money charged upon land is secured by an express trust?

A. Not after 1st January, 1879, by the Real Property Limitation Act, 1874.

Q. What becomes of unclaimed dividends on stock, if not claimed for ten years?

A. Such stock, together with the unclaimed dividends, is transferred to the account of the Commissioners for the Reduction of the National Debt; and such dividends, together with all the future dividends on the stock, are invested by the commissioners in the purchase of like stock, so as to accumulate. And the governor, or deputy-governor for the time being, may order the transfer of such stock, and the payment of the dividends to any person proving his right to the same. If the governor or deputy-governor is not satisfied of the legality of the claim, an order for transfer and payment may be obtained from the Chancery Division of the High Court by petition, in a summary way, stating and verifying the claim.

Q. In case of the assignment of a chose in action, should any notice be given to the transferee?

A. When a chose in action, either legal or equitable, is transferred from one person to another, notice of the assignment should be given by the transferee to the person liable to the action at law or suit in equity, the right to bring which is the subject of the transfer. Thus, if a debt be assigned, notice of the assignment should be given to the debtor. Every person about to take an assignment of a chose in action should inquire of the person liable to the action or suit whether he has notice of any prior assignment. In order to obtain a good title he must himself give notice to the person or one of the persons liable to the debt or demand assigned to him. When this has been done his title will be secure, and will prevail over that of any unknown prior assignee who may have omitted to give such notice.

Q. What is a stop order, and what is the effect of it?

A. If the property (alluded to in the last answer) consist of money or stock standing in the name of the paymaster-general, or of securities in his possession, an order of the court should be obtained, restraining transfer or payment without notice to the assignee. This order is called a *stop order*, and will have the same effect as notice of an assignment given to any private debtor. If it be stock standing in the name of a trustee who is dead with a representative, a distringas to restrain the transfer of the stock will confer the same priority as notice to the trustee if living.

Q. Is an intermediate trustee now necessary on an assignment of personal estate by a person to himself and another?

A. No; the statute 22 & 23 Vict. c. 35, s. 21, provides that any person shall have power to assign personal property, now by law assignable, directly to himself and another person or persons or corporations by the like means as he might assign the same to another.

Q. What difference is there in the settlement of real and settlement of personal property?

A. Lands, unlike stock, may be converted from arable

to pasture, may be cut up into roads, canals or railways, may be sold for building purposes, let upon lease, disposed of by contingent remainders, shifting uses and executory devises, without the intervention of any trustees. Personal property, on the contrary, cannot be settled without the intervention of trustees, in whom a great degree of personal confidence must necessarily be placed; but when so settled the title to it is sometimes as long and intricate as that to real estate.

www.ingramcontent.com/pod-product-compliance
Lightning Source LLC
Chambersburg PA
CBHW030616270326
41927CB00007B/1196